Series Editors
Joan Kang Shin
JoAnn (Jodi) Crandall

Author
Kate Cory-Wright

NATIONAL GEOGRAPHIC LEARNING

Australia • Brazil • Japan • Korea • Mexico • Singapore • Spain • United Kingdom • United States

Unit 1

Exciting Sports

1 **Do the puzzle.** Find the secret message.

accident	height	skillfully
are	injury	strength
cool	kite surfing	to crash
equipment	length	to flip
extreme sports	motocross	to land
~~hang-gliding~~	skiing	to travel

1. Cross out the names of four sports.
2. Cross out four actions.
3. Cross out the nouns formed from *long, strong* and *high.*
4. Cross out all the words with three syllables (e.g., *e-quip-ment*).

Read the words that you didn't cross out. Write the message:

____

2 **Look and write.** Complete the sentences.

1. The ____height____ of this bike is ____86 cm (34 inches)____.
2. If you buy a BMX bike, you should always check the ______________ of the "top tube." The top tube is the bar that goes from the handlebars to the seat.
3. The ______________ of this bike's top tube is ______________.
4. The boy's ______________ is ______________. He's the tallest boy in my class.

3 Describe the pictures.

do motocross	crash	along the sea	equipment
go hang-gliding	flip	in a field	injury
go kite surfing	land	in the air	skillful
go skiing	travel	into a rock	strength

1. He's doing motocross. He's crashing into a rock. He may have an injury.
2. ______________________________
3. ______________________________
4. ______________________________

4 Read and match the questions and answers.

1. My favorite sport is surfing. What about you?
2. Have you ever had an accident while playing sports?
3. What kind of equipment do you need for swimming?
4. I love to watch extreme sports on TV. Those athletes are so skillful.
5. What's the worst injury you've ever had?

a. I agree. I like how some of them flip in the air before landing.
b. Yes, a year ago. I crashed into a rock on my bike and broke my arm.
c. I've broken a finger, but that's all. I've been very lucky!
d. Nothing expensive—just a swimsuit.
e. I like skateboarding best of all, but I'm not very good at it!

5 **Listen and speak.** Check your answers to Activity 4. Then listen and repeat. **TR: 02**

6 **Look and listen.** Check the sports that the singer has dreamed of doing. **TR: 03**

1 ☑ 2 ☐ 3 ☐

4 ☐ 5 ☐ 6 ☐

7 **Listen.** Listen to a part of the song. Write three of the rhyming words in the chorus. **TR: 04**

air care compare everywhere pair wear

Extreme sports.
Flying high in the ____________!
Other sports
don't ____________!

Extreme sports.
Look around.
They're ____________!

8 **Work with a partner.** Write a new chorus. Make an acrostic poem!

S ______________________________

P ______________________________

O ______________________________

R ______________________________

T ______________________________

S ______________________________

GRAMMAR

I **have lived** in this house **since** 2001. /**Since** 2001, I have lived in this house.

They **have not been** to this school **since** December.

SINCE + *point in time*

We **have not been** hang-gliding **for** three months.

She **has taken** classes **for** five years.

FOR + *length of time*

9 Read and write. Look at the timeline. Write the sentences.

1960s · 1970s · 2000 · 2008 · Today

SINCE + point in time

1. Motocross / be / an Olympic sport / 2008.
   Motocross has been an Olympic sport since 2008.
2. People / enjoy / kite boarding / the year 2000.
3. Surfing / be popular / around the world / the 1970s.
4. 1960s / more than 10 million people / try / skateboarding.

10 Read and write. Read the sentences in Activity 9 and do the math! Rewrite the sentences.

1. Motocross has been an Olympic sport for more than five years.
2. ______
3. ______
4. ______

11 Work with a partner. Say the sentences two different ways.

I'll start. "Surfing has been popular around the world since the 1970s."

My turn. "Surfing has been popular around the world for forty years."

12 **Look and find.** Look at the photos. Which ones have the following equipment?

brakes	elbow pads	a helmet	knee pads	a life jacket
b,	______	________	______	______

13 **Work with a partner.** Discuss the pictures.

1. What is the boy doing to his brakes? Why are brakes so important?
2. How many people are wearing helmets?
3. What is the skateboarder wearing for protection? How will they protect him?
4. What color are most life jackets? Why?

14 **Listen.** Circle the safety equipment that Carla can borrow. **TR: 05**

a helmet   a life jacket   brakes   elbow pads   knee pads

15 **Listen again.** Complete the conversation. **TR: 06**

Carla: I'm going on an extreme sports course next weekend!
____

Alex: Of course you can. ____

Carla: That's a good idea. Thanks, Alex.

Alex: No problem!

Carla: Um, we're also going kitesurfing. ______________________________

Alex: ____________________ It's brand new. I've only had it for three days!

Carla: That's okay. I understand.

16 **Complete the text.** Do the crossword.

Every year, extreme sports such as hang-gliding and **(9 down)** ______ become more popular. Many young people want to **(5 down)** ______ through the air on a board or bike. People also want to fly to greater heights and **(6 across)** ______. Unfortunately, too many people fall or **(2 across)** ______. Every year, there are more **(10 across)** ______ from broken bones, or worse. How can we prevent so many bad **(3 down)** ______? Here is some advice:

1. Do not copy what you see on TV or in videos. Those people are **(4 across)** ______ at their sports because they have practiced for years. Be patient!
2. Learn how to **(6 down)** ______. If you can do that skillfully, then you may not hurt yourself.
3. Build up your physical **(1 down)** ______ slowly.
4. Take classes. Learn how to go kite surfing or **(7 down)** ______.
5. Wear proper **(8 across)** ______: helmets, knee pads, and life jackets.

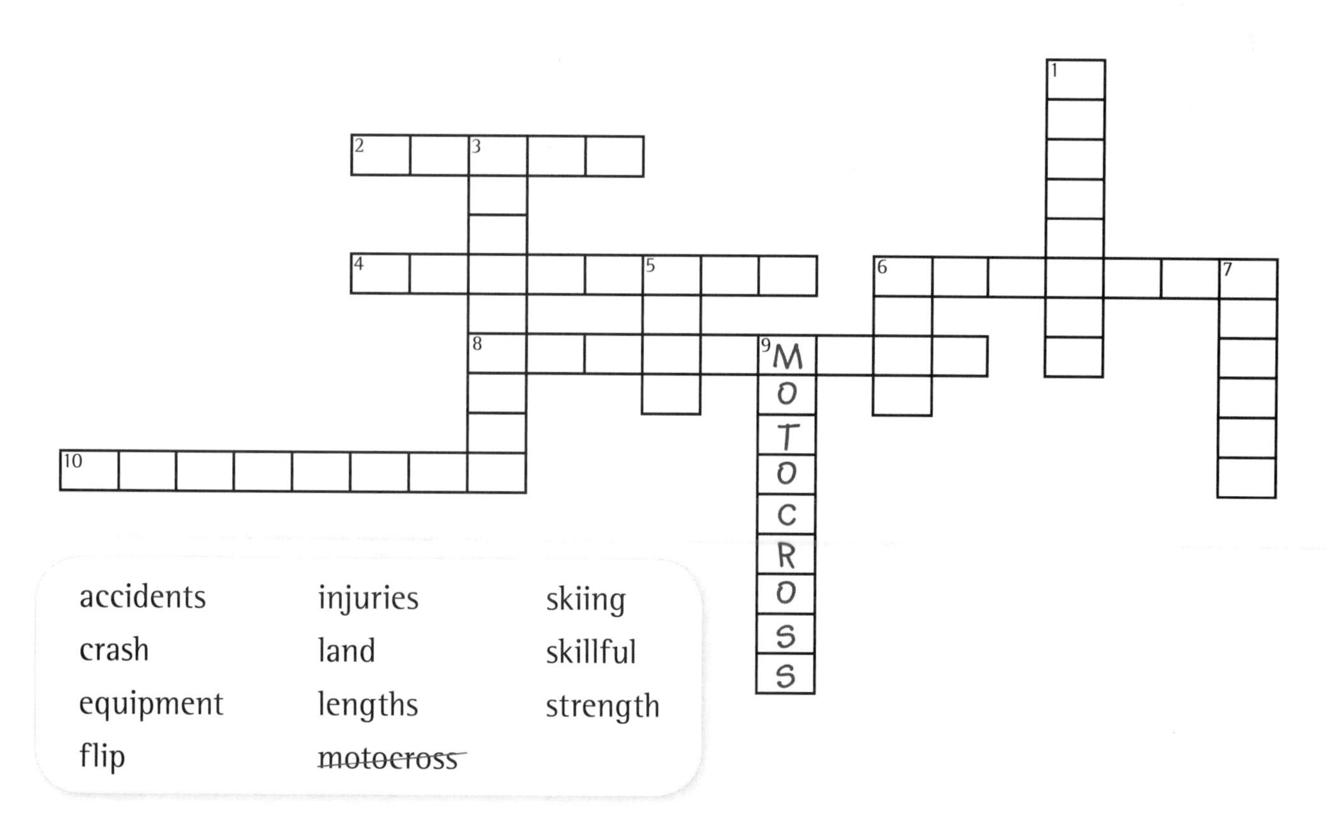

MOTOCROSS
accidents
crash
equipment
flip
injuries
land
lengths
~~motocross~~
skiing
skillful
strength

GRAMMAR

I think skiing is	extremely	boring.
That sport is	incredibly	cool.
Those tricks look	really	dangerous.
That boy's life jacket looks	so	difficult.
	super	exciting.
	totally	fun.
	very	scary.
		silly.

17 Write and speak. Write your opinions. Then compare them with a partner's opinions. Do you agree?

1. A sport that looks really dangerous:

____

2. A famous person who looks totally cool:

____

3. A school subject that is extremely difficult:

____

4. A relative or friend who is super fun: ________________________________

5. A vacation that was very exciting: ________________________________

18 What about you? What is your favorite or least favorite thing? Why? Write five true sentences in your notebook. Share your answers with a partner.

extreme sport	so	movie	totally	book
incredibly	TV program	extremely	musical group	super

19 **Read and write.** Write the expressions in the chart.

last night	ten years	2012
a long time	we were six	about twenty years

A point in time	A length of time
2000 / the 1970s / May / Monday	two days / three weeks / a year
___	___
___	___
___	___

20 **Read and circle the correct words.** Then listen and check your answers. **TR: 07**

1. I've known my best friend **for / since** ten years.
2. We've studied at the same school **for / since** we were six years old.
3. Our parents have been friends **for / since** about twenty years!
4. We've spent our vacations together **for / since** 2012.
5. We used to fight a lot, but we haven't fought **for / since** a long time!

21 **Write in your notebook.** Answer the questions with two sentences. Use *for* and *since*.

How long have you done these things? How do you like them?

have a bicycle	so
have a skateboard	extremely
know your sports teacher	incredibly
live in your house	really
study English	very

22 **Listen and read.** TR: 08

An Extreme Challenge

Many people think extreme sports are new, but are they really? In fact, some sports have existed for a long time but have only become famous recently. For example, the Hawaiian people used to surf back in 400 B.C.E. Their boards were made of wood. Although they invented surfing, it didn't become a well-known sport until the 1970s. Similarly, the popular extreme sport "free running" has existed for centuries in Africa, but no one gave it a name until recently.

In addition, some extreme sports that we consider new are simply a combination of two older sports. For example, surfing and kite flying are ancient sports. However, when surfers began to use kites, another extreme sport was born: kite surfing. We have also created sports such as sand boarding, snowboarding, skydiving, waterskiing, and wingsuit flying. Can you guess what they are? Look closely at their names.

Humans have done extreme sports for centuries, and we will continue. New technology and equipment will help us go higher, faster, deeper, and farther. We will create more ideas, too. Think about "extreme ironing" (ironing clothes while you dive underwater or climb a mountain). We don't need to iron clothes underwater, so why do people do extreme ironing? Humans love a challenge!

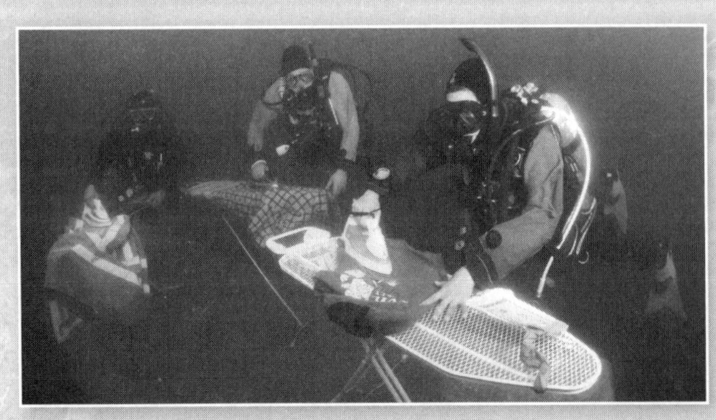

Three men played the cello on top of the four tallest mountains in Scotland, England, Wales, and Ireland. They called it "extreme cello playing."

23 **Read the text again.** Check the main idea in each paragraph.

1. ☐ a. Surfing and free running are very old sports.
   ☐ b. Extreme sports are not new.
2. ☐ a. We can adapt old sports to make new ones.
   ☐ b. We can guess the meaning of some sports if we look at their names.
3. ☐ a. Humans like to discover new things.
   ☐ b. Extreme ironing is not necessary, but it is fun.

24 **Determine meaning.** Find these extreme sports in the text. What do you think they are? Write them in the box.

Extreme sports	Water sport	Land sport	Air sport
kite surfing			
sand boarding			
snow boarding			
skydiving			
waterskiing			
wingsuit flying			

25 **Work with a partner.** Invent another type of extreme sport for the future. Take notes. Describe it to the class.

____

____

____

____

____

____

26 **Read *High Climber* on page 16 of your Student Book.** How did the writer plan her writing? Read the steps.

1. First, the writer chose someone interesting.

   Quickly read the text about Moniz. What are the three most interesting facts, in your opinion? Write them in your notebook.

2. Next, the writer found out about Matt Moniz's life and wrote down ideas for her biography. She used a timeline.

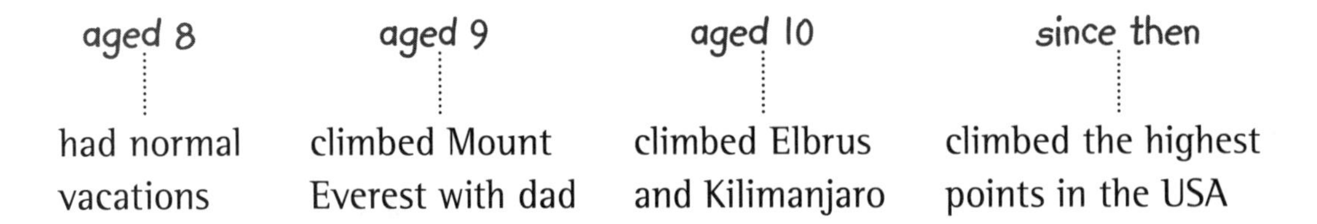

3. After reading her notes, she tried to make it more interesting for the reader by connecting the dates and events in Matt's life.

   Match the events and dates in Matt's life. Draw lines.

   1. Before the age of nine, Matt Moniz enjoyed summer vacations
   2. Then suddenly his life
   3. At the time, Matt did not know
   4. After that, there was no
   5. In 2010, Matt became the youngest person

   a. changed.
   b. stopping him!
   c. like all kids do.
   d. in the world to . . .
   e. what to expect.

4. Then, she thought of words and expressions that show time: *after (that), before, since then, the next year, then, at the time, suddenly, afterward.*

   Read the sentences in Activity 3 again. In your notebook, write the time expressions she uses.

5. Finally, she wrote her first version, called a draft, of her paragraph.

27 **What do you remember about Danny MacAskill and Bethany Hamilton? Write information in the chart.** Read *Cool Adventurers* on page 14 of your Student Book if you need help with the dates and details.

Danny MacAskill	Bethany Hamilton
Born in Scotland in 1985	Born in Hawaii in . . .
A cyclist who flips off buildings and rides a bike on a train	A surfer who . . .
Has had a few accidents and has broken twelve helmets and a few bones	She had an accident when . . .
A video of him was on YouTube in 2009	
"National Geographer Adventurer of the Year" in 2012	

28 **Write sentences about Danny and Bethany.** Use the chart and expressions of time.

1. Danny began extreme cycling when he was a kid. Since then, he has broken twelve helmets.
2. ________________
3. ________________
4. ________________
5. ________________

29 **Now follow steps 1-5 on page 12.** Write your paragraph about Danny or Bethany in your notebook.

30 **Express yourself.** Choose someone who you find interesting, and write a biography of him or her. Plan your writing, and follow the steps on page 12. Write your new paragraph in your notebook.

Unit 2

History's a Mystery

1 Do the puzzle. Find the secret message.

Scrambled	Answer	Numbers
DEID	d i e d	6
NYALAZE		5
DUIBER		11 20
VEHSETI		12 14
TEUTAS		15
RULRE		4 1
TTAOOT		13
OLGD		7
MYMMU		22
SAECU		8 21
REPVRSEE		16 18 2
MOTB		19
TEACAVXE		3 17
CEOBTJ		10 9

analyze	object
buried	preserve
cause	ruler
~~died~~	statue
excavate	tattoo
gold	thieves
mummy	tomb

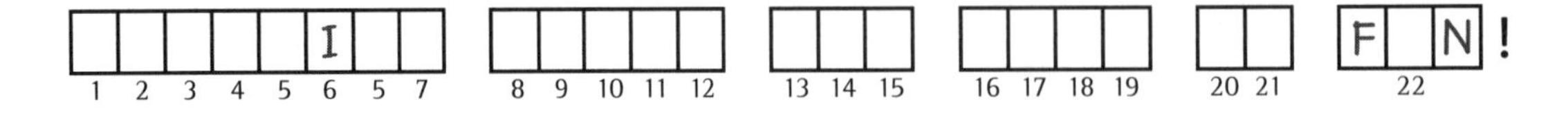

2 Label the pictures.

1. objects

2. s

3. t

4. t

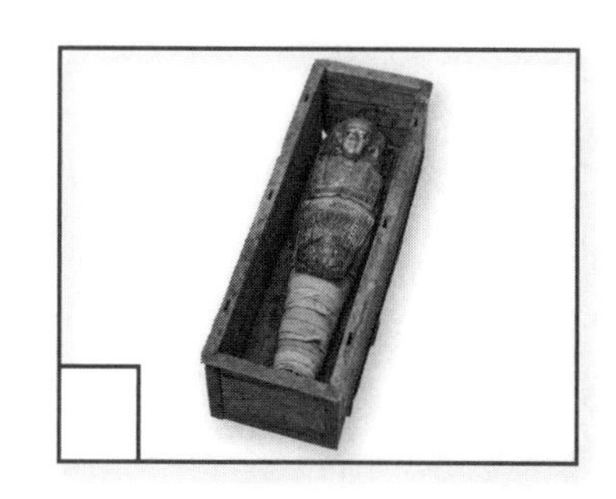

5. m

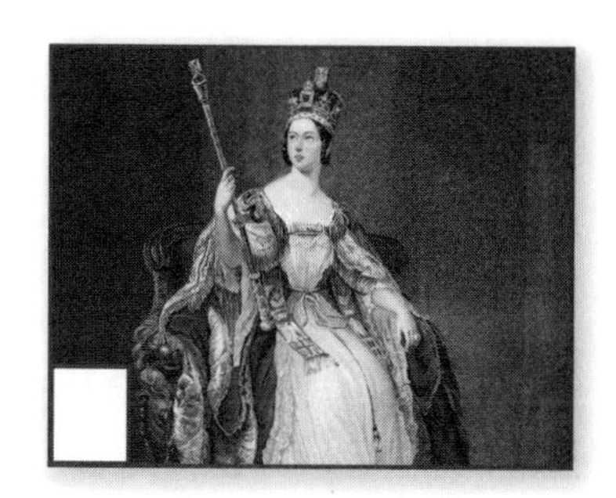

6. r

3 **Listen.** Check the words in Activity 2 that you hear. **TR: 09**

4 **Listen to track 9 again.** Check **T** for *True* and **F** for *False*.

1. Mei went to a museum on the weekend.	T	F ✓
2. Thieves stole the statues.	T	F
3. She saw three mummies.	T	F
4. The treasure was in the tomb.	T	F
5. The ruler had tattoos on his arms.	T	F
6. There was very little gold and treasure.	T	F

5 **Work with a partner.** Discuss the questions.

1. Would you like to be a rich ruler with lots of treasure? Why or why not?
2. What would you do if you discovered a tomb by accident?
3. Would you like to be an archaeologist? Why or why not?

6 **Listen to the song.** Number the words in the order that you first hear them (1–5). **TR: 10**

☐ a. scientists

☐ b. mummies

☐ c. money

☐ d. pottery

1 f. statues

7 **Read the verses.** Find a word or phrase that means the same. Then listen to the song in track 10 again.

Excavated (1) ***kings***
were found by (2) ***archaeologists***
Anglo Saxon (3) ***treasure***
was (4) ***discovered***
in the mist.

The Terracotta (5) ***Army***
was found deep underground.
Just (6) ***think*** *what you might find*
if you look around.

☐ to have in mind
1 rulers
☐ found
☐ gold objects and money
☐ group of soldiers
☐ people who study the past

8 **Work with a partner.** Discuss the questions.

1. Imagine you are an archaeologist. What would you like to find?
2. Why does the singer think that history is interesting? Do you agree?
3. What mysteries does the singer mention? What do you know about them?

GRAMMAR

I He/She/It You We They People	**was** **were**	not	hurt in an accident. given a gift. discovered. stolen. given homework. sent to bed.	**wasn't** = was not **weren't** = were not
When Where	**were** **was**	you it	born? found?	

9 **Look and write.** Complete the sentences.

be born ~~bury~~ call find give hide

1. The coins were buried in a hole in the ground.

   The police think they ________ many years ago by thieves.

2. A cat ________ up a tree this morning.

   The firefighters ________. They came and saved it.

3. My daughter ________ on my birthday.

   I ________ the best birthday present in the world: a daughter!

10 **What about you?** Make five questions. Then answer with true sentences in your notebook.

1. When were you born? (be born)
2. ________ you ________ something cute when you were a kid? (call)
3. As a child, ________ you ________ a special gift that you still have? (give)
4. ________ you ever ________ to bed early because you were naughty? (send)

11 Match the words to the definitions.

an artifact   a CT scan   a DNA test   a sample   a site

1. __________ is a place that archaeologists want to excavate or explore.
2. __________ is an object found at the site. It is not a living thing. It was made by someone.
3. __________ is a way to discover what is in the body's cells. It can help you find your relatives.
4. __________ is a way to see inside a body. You can discover if a person has illnesses.
5. __________ is a small amount of something, such as food, that someone analyzes.

12 **Listen and write.** How do we know so much about the Iceman? Listen to the archaeologist. Write a word from Activity 11. TR: 11

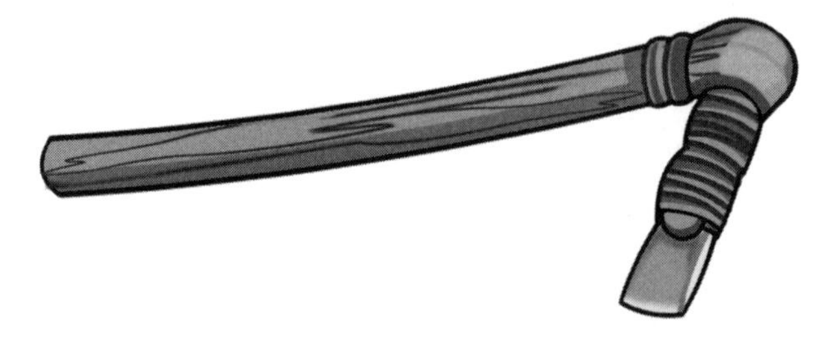

1. The Iceman wasn't a very important man, but he was quite rich. __________
2. His last meal was cereal and meat. __________
3. He climbed the mountain before he died. __________
4. He had three different illnesses before he went on the journey. __________
5. He didn't die from an illness. He died from an arrow in his left shoulder.

____

13 **What about you?** Write a short paragraph in your notebook.

Which famous archaeological site in the world would you really like to visit? Why? Where is it? What can you see and do there?

artifact   buried   died   discover   site

14 **Read.** Complete each sentence. Circle the correct words in the text.

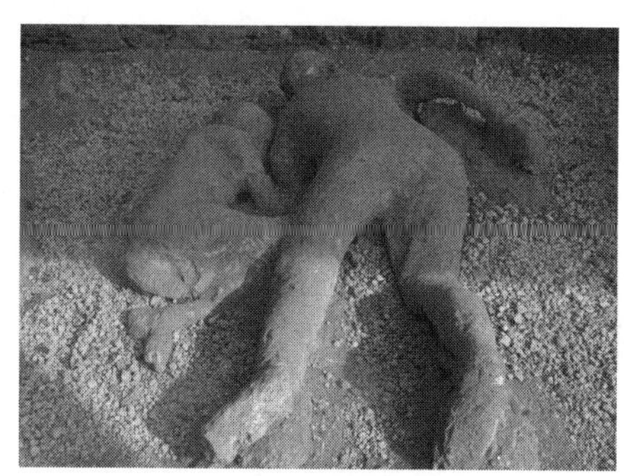

Pompeii, Italy

In 79 B.C.E., over 16,000 people **died / analyzed** in one night. The **CT scan / cause** was a terrible volcano. When Mount Vesuvius erupted, the people of Pompeii were quickly **excavated / buried** under volcanic ash. After the volcano, Pompeii was forgotten for nearly 1,700 years. Then, in 1748, it was **discovered / died** by chance. When the ruins were **excavated / preserved**, many people were found still in bed or eating at the table! Thanks to the ash, most things were perfectly **preserved / analyzed**. The ash also prevented **thieves / samples** from stealing treasure. Scientists have **analyzed / buried** samples of the people's food, and they have studied many **artifacts / DNA tests**, such as clothes and paintings. Most **gold / objects** are in museums, so we can see how the people of Pompeii lived thousands of years ago!

15 **Read and write.** Imagine your friend went to Pompeii on vacation. Prepare six questions in your notebook.

How many people died in Pompeii?

16 **Work with a partner.** Ask and answer questions. Take turns.

How was your vacation to Pompeii?

Awesome! We learned all about the people who were buried that night.

Why were they buried? What happened?

GRAMMAR

Pompeii The treasure The pictures These games	**was** **were**	**discovered** **stolen** **drawn** **created**	**by**	a hiker. thieves. artists. the children.
Was **Were**	the cat it the photos the letters	**saved** **found** **taken** **sent**		firefighters? the police? a friend? a neighbor?
Who	**was**	the Iceman	**found**	**by**?

17 **Read and write.** Use *by* only when it is necessary.

Around 246 B.C.E, about 700,000 men were hired by (hire) the Chinese ruler Qin Shi Huang to make an army of men. He wanted the army to protect him after he died. For nearly forty years, thousands of statues ________________ (make) the men. When the ruler died in 210 B.C.E, the statues ________________ (bury) with him in a tomb. This incredible treasure ________________ (forget) for centuries, but in 1974 it ________________ (find) Chinese farmers! When the site ________________ (excavate) archaeologists a few years later, more than 6,000 statues ________________ (discover). There were soldiers, horses, musicians, and acrobats! Originally, the statues ________________ (paint) in different colors, but now the colors have gone. All the same, they are beautiful, because each statue is *different*! Can you see the differences?

18 **Listen.** Listen to Martha talk about the project. Who did what? Draw lines. **TR: 12**

Soldiers	Alex
Artifacts	Ben
Text	Martha
Photo	Suzy
Horse	

19 **Write questions.**

1. These Terracotta soldiers are awesome! They / make / Ben?

   Were they made by Ben?

2. What about the artifacts? They / paint / Alex?

   ____

3. The text is very good. It / write / Suzy?

   ____

4. I love the photo. It / take / the teacher?

   ____

5. What about the horse? It / buy or make / Martha?

   ____

20 **Write.** Describe some favorite objects in your home.

In our living room there is an old book. It was written by my grandfather.

____

____

____

____

____

21 **Listen and read.** TR: 13

Trash Is Treasure

All archaeologists study human history, but there are many kinds of archaeologists. Forensic archaeologists analyze DNA and help police with crimes. Landscape archaeologists study sites. Osteologists are interested in bones. What about Dr. Rathje? He was a "garbologist." That means he studied trash. From the 1970s to the 1990s, he excavated twenty-one landfills and analyzed the contents of more than fourteen tons of waste material. Studying waste was fascinating to him.

Garbology is an important part of archaeology. In some ancient civilizations, such as Pompeii and Herculaneum, everything was buried. There was nothing left behind, no writing, tombs, or artifacts. To learn more about the population, archaeologists had to study trash left behind. When 774 sacks of trash were excavated in Herculaneum, the 2,000-year-old remains showed us what objects people threw away, as well as what food they ate and diseases they had.

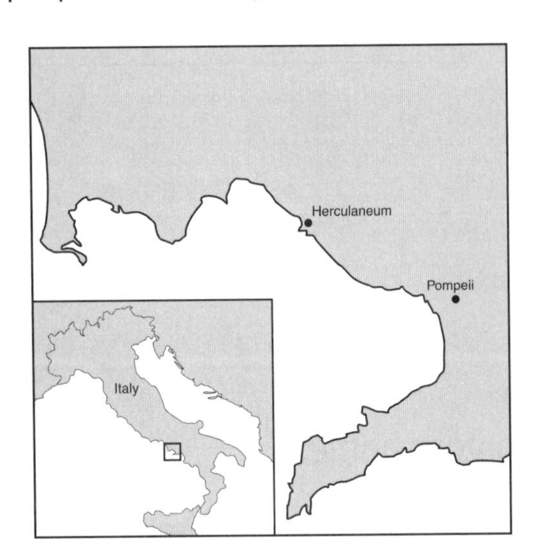

Biodegradable trash from the past is still useful today. Dr. Rathje discovered that biodegradable trash buried underground does not decompose as quickly as we thought. In 1989, a newspaper from 1952 was dug up by his team, and it was perfectly preserved. They could still read it! Similarly, old grass found by his team was still green, and a hot dog found in a landfill still looked good enough to eat. Would you like to be a garbologist?

22 **Check T for *True* and F for *False*.**

1. Not all archaeologists work at ancient sites. T 
2. Only non-biodegradable trash helps us learn about the past.  F
3. Biodegradable trash decomposes quickly when it is buried.  

23 **Read again.** Reread the first paragraph. Label the tree. Write one key word in each circle.

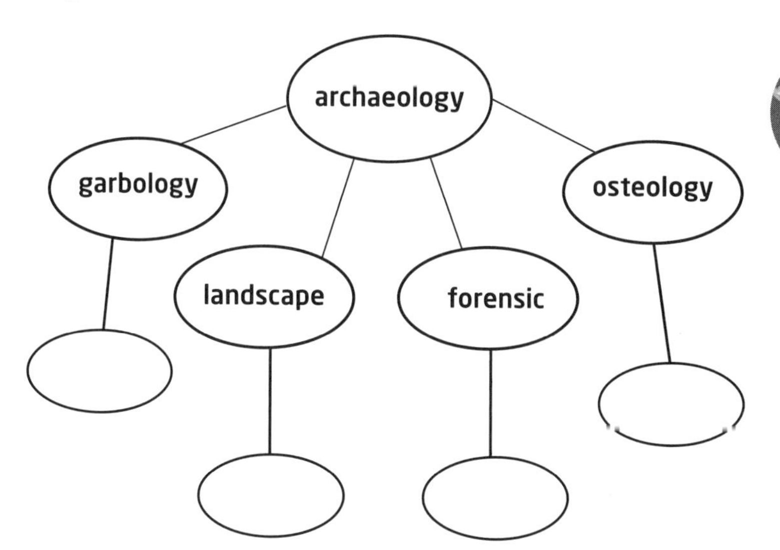

Archaeologists studying trash discovered in Herculaneum found lost jewelry, coins, and semi-precious stones!

24 **Read and discuss.** Check the main idea in each paragraph. How did you find your answers? Where do we usually find the main idea in paragraphs?

Paragraph 1

a. ☐ Archaeology has many purposes, but it is basically about studying human history.

b. ☐ From the 1970s to the 1990s, Dr. Rathje excavated 21 landfills.

Paragraph 2

a. ☐ Trash found in Herculaneum told us a lot about the population.

b. ☐ Garbology is important in the world of archaeology.

Paragraph 3

a. ☐ Waste from the past can help us a lot today.

b. ☐ Dr. Rathje made an important discovery about biodegradable waste.

25 **Work with a partner.** Discuss different kinds of archaeologists (forensic, landscape, garbologist, osteologist). Think of two advantages and disadvantages of each job.

26 Read *Memories from the Past* on page 32 of your Student Book.

How did the writer plan her writing? Read the steps.

1. First, the writer chose a main theme or argument.

   Each new discovery tells us about the past.

2. Next, the writer used a T-chart to plan her writing. She wrote down the discoveries of two mummies. She listed general things that the two mummies taught us (or her) about the past.

Iceman mummy	Peruvian mummy
how people lived	how people were buried, and who with
what people ate, used, and wore	who had tattoos
illnesses people had	

3. After reading about the Peruvian mummy and the Iceman, she wrote down specific *examples of new things* she learned from each discovery. She added this information to her T-chart.

Iceman mummy	Peruvian mummy
How people lived Example: they hunted	How people were buried, and who with Example: men were buried with important women
What people ate, used, and wore Example: expensive axes	Who had tattoos Example: women had tattoos (not just men)
Illnesses people had Example: bad teeth, stomach problems	

4. Then, she thought of words and expressions to introduce examples:

   for instance, such as, namely, specifically, a good example is . . .

   Find the expressions that the writer used in these sentences. Copy them from the text. Pay attention to punctuation.

a. A good example is ____ the famous Iceman mummy discovered in 1991 by hikers.

b. We know more about people who lived long ago, ________________ what they wore and how they lived.

c. ________________, we know that women were given tattoos.

d. We still don't know everything about these mummies (________________, the cause of their death).

5. Finally, she wrote her first version, called a draft, of her paragraph. Now it's time to plan your own writing.

27 Complete the chart. What do you remember about King Tut's tomb and the Terracotta statues? Read page 22 and pages 30-31 in your Student Book if you need help.

	King Tut's Tomb	Terracotta statues
When and where?	1328 B.C.E - Egypt	210 B.C.E - China
Who was the tomb for?		the Chinese ruler, Qin Shi Huang Di
What was buried with him?		
Why?	to take to his next life	

28 Now follow steps on pages 24-25. Write your paragraph in your notebook. Use words and expressions that show exemplification.

29 Express yourself. Choose from the topics below, and write a paragraph of exemplification. Plan your writing, and follow the steps on pages 24-25. Write your paragraph in your notebook.

Write about one place in your country that archaeologists think is important. Include examples.

Write about your favorite archaeological site in the world. Include examples.

Unit 3

Chocolate!

1 **Read and write.** Complete the sentences. Then do the puzzle.

			1.	P	O	W	D	E	R
	2.						E		
	3.						L		
			4.				I		
				5.			C		
		6.					I		
7.							O		
			8.				U		
			9.				S		

1. Cocoa ______ is dry, but you can drink it if you add hot milk.
2. ______ and strawberry are my two favorite fillings.
3. I think that ______ is a boring flavor, but it tastes good in ice cream.
4. The opposite of liquid is ______.
5. The ______ tree grows near the equator.
6. Do you know the ______ of chocolate? It's from the Americas!
7. This kind of spice smells nice. It's brown and it's called ______.
8. In the Americas, chocolate wasn't eaten. It was drunk as a ______.
9. Cacao ______ contain many seeds. One has enough for seven candy bars!

2 **Write.** Answer the questions.

1. Can you name two types of chocolate liquid drinks?

   Chocolate milk shake and hot chocolate.

2. Have you ever smelled or tasted cinnamon? What was it like?

   ___

3. How often do you eat chocolate? Which are your two favorite fillings?

   ___

4. What's the difference between cocoa and cacao?

   ___

5. Look at two objects near you. Where were they made? Can you find the origin?

   ___

3 **Work with a partner.** Complete and write the questions. Write your answers. Write your partner's answers.

	You	Your partner
1. What's / your / favorite type / ice cream?	___	___
2. How many / candy bars / you / eat / every week?	___	___
3. you/ ever / drink / hot chocolate?	___	___
4. you/ know / how to make / milk shake?	___	___

4 **Discuss as a group.** How are your answers similar and different?

Mario and Paolo never drink hot chocolate, but I like it!

5 Match the words and the pictures.

a cup heat it up pour spice sprinkle stir

a. pour

b. ______

c. ______

d. ______

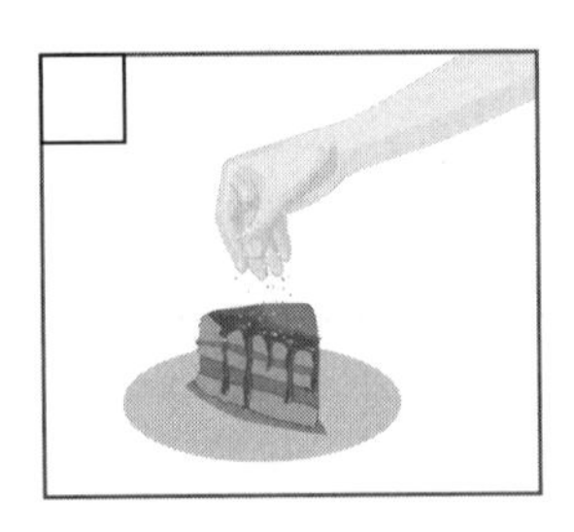

e. ______

f. ______

6 **Listen to the song.** As you listen, number the order (1-6) that you hear the actions in Activity 5. TR: 14

7 **Listen and write.** Listen to the song. Answer the questions. TR: 15

1. Where and when was the singer making hot chocolate?

______

2. Was her grandma telling her she was doing it right?

______

3. Who was making cocoa when she was young?

______

4. Was her grandma telling her to stand up?

______

GRAMMAR

I He / She / It	**was**	not	**swimming**. **skateboarding**. **playing** soccer. **eating** ice cream. **taking** hang-gliding classes.
You We They People	**were**		
What Where Why	**was** **were**	he / she / it you	**doing**? **thinking**? **going**? **singing**?

8 **Write.** Write the *-ing* form of the verbs.

1. eat ___________
2. live ___________
3. win ___________
4. make ___________
5. swim ___________
6. sleep ___________

9 **Complete the sentences.** Then listen and check your answers. **TR: 16**

Mom: What ___were you doing___ (you / do) last night, Sarah?

Sarah: What do you mean, Mom? I ______________ (sleep)!

Dad: No, you ______________ (not). I heard you. You ______________ (walk) around the house at 3 a.m.

Son: I heard her, too, Dad. She ______________ (make) a noise in the kitchen.

Mom: I don't understand. Why ______________ (you / make) a noise downstairs, Sarah?

Sarah: I ______________ (make) a . . . CAKE! Happy Birthday, Mom!

10 **What about you?** Write what you were doing at these times.

1. At 8 p.m. last night, I ______________________________.
2. Half an hour ago, I ______________________________.
3. I ______________________________ when the cell phone rang.
4. Once, I broke a bone! I ______________________________ at the time.

11 **Listen.** Listen to the story. Number the words in the order you hear them. **TR: 17**

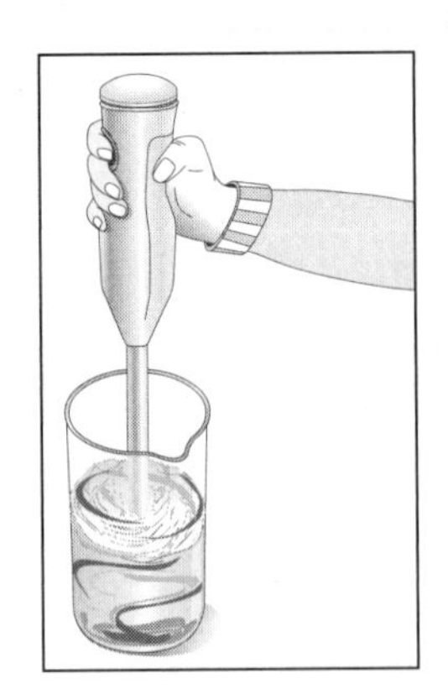

☐	grams	☐	ingredients	☐	mix
1	recipe	☐	teaspoons		

12 **Listen to the rest of the story.** Circle the correct answers. **TR: 18**

1. What are they making?
   a. chocolate ice cream b. a chocolate milk shake

2. Why can't they pour it?
   a. It's too thick. b. They can't find the glasses.

3. What was the mistake?
   a. They didn't mix it enough. b. They didn't add enough milk.

13 **Match the questions and answers.**

1. I'm so excited. I really want to drink this chocolate milk shake!
2. Where's the recipe?
3. So, do we have all the ingredients?
4. How many teaspoons of cocoa powder should I put in?
5. Should I pour it now?

a. Six is fine. Then mix it with the ice cream and the milk.
b. Me too. I haven't had one for months!
c. It's here. I put it in front of us so we can see it.
d. Sure. Here are the glasses.
e. I think so. We have milk, ice cream, and cocoa powder.

14 **Read the banana milk shake recipe**. Underline the correct words.

Print the *menu* / *recipe* for the banana milk shake. Check that you have all the *ingredients* / *pods*. Put the milk, ice cream, banana, and a *solid* / *teaspoon* of sugar in the blender. Mix everything together for one minute. Pour the *grams* / *liquid* into two glasses.

15 **Which word doesn't belong?** Underline the "odd word out."

1. milk shake	hot chocolate	recipe	cocoa powder
2. cinnamon	solid	sugar	spice
3. teaspoon	fork	candy bar	knife
4. Spanish	Belgian	origin	English
5. gram	cacao	pod	seed
6. mix	discover	pour	add
7. chocolate	vanilla	liquid	strawberry
8. ingredients	dark chocolate	white chocolate	milk chocolate

16 **Read.** Circle the correct word.

Chocolate has changed a lot since it was first introduced by the people of the Americas. At that time, all *cacao / cocoa* trees were grown in the Americas, but now most cacao *pods / origin* come from West Africa. In addition, chocolate used to be a *spice / liquid* that people drank. They didn't have *hot chocolate / candy bars.*

Today, we usually eat chocolate in a solid form. The *caramel / ingredients* have changed. Thousands of years ago, chocolate was usually made from *recipe / cocoa* and water, mixed with honey and peppers. Since then, we have added sugar, vanilla, and spices such as *cinnamon / powder.* Of course, now we have chocolate with strawberry or caramel *fillings / types* inside them. Mmmm. Now I'm hungry!

17 **Work with a partner.** Compare your answers. Then discuss the main differences.

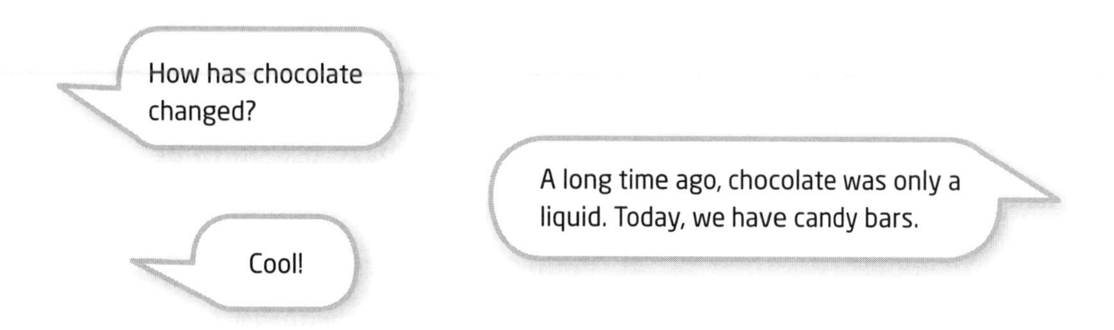

How has chocolate changed?
A long time ago, chocolate was only a liquid. Today, we have candy bars.
Cool!

GRAMMAR

Present tense		
Let's put the recipe here	so (that)	we **can** see it.
I think we need to add more sugar		it **tastes** sweeter.
Past tense		
Jun-Uh put the recipe in front of her	so (that)	she **could** see it.
We added some milk		the ice cream **would** taste better.
We put the cake in the fridge		it **wouldn't** melt.

18 Complete the sentences.

1. I printed out the recipe so that we ___could read___ it before we cooked. (can / read)
2. We put some cinnamon on the banana milk shake so that it ________________ more interesting. (will / taste)
3. We used a blender so that we ________________ the ingredients more quickly. (can / mix)
4. Sarah made a cake at night so that her mom ________________ a surprise the next day. (will / have)
5. I did my homework in the afternoon so that I ________________ later. (can / watch TV)
6. Sarah hid the cake so that her mom ________________ it. (will not / see)

19 **Read and write.** Match the cause and effect.

a saucer

a coffee house

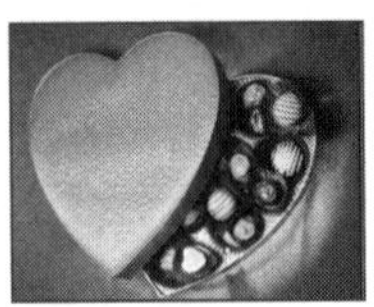

a box of candy

a wrapper

brownies

Cause	**Effect**
1. saucers	a. The chocolate didn't get dirty.
2. coffee houses	b. People could make brownies at home.
3. candy boxes	c. Hot liquids didn't fall on clothes.
4. candy wrappers	d. People could meet to have a drink and talk.
5. recipes for brownies	e. We can send chocolate to people we love.

20 **Write.** Complete the sentences.

1. Saucers were invented ______________________________.
2. Coffee houses were built ______________________________.
3. Candy boxes were made ______________________________.
4. Candy wrappers were used ______________________________.
5. Brownie recipes were published in magazines ______________________________

______________________________.

21 **Listen and write.** Listen. Complete the chart. **TR: 19**

What was happening in the pictures?	Why?
1. The boy was wearing a huge hat	so that he wouldn't get sunburned.
2. He was carrying a big map	so that ______________________________.
3. He ______________________________	so that he could learn how it is made.
4. She ______________________________	so that everyone ______________________________.

22 **Work with a partner.** Student 1, go to page 122. Student 2, go to page 124.

23 Listen and read. TR: 20

The Sweet World of Art

Italian Mirco Della Vecchia, born in 1980, is both a chef and an artist. In fact, he's a "chocolatier." Since he was thirteen years old, Vecchia has known how to make delicious dishes from chocolate, and he has won many prizes for his awesome ice creams and chocolate cakes. From 1994 until 2000, he worked in famous chocolate stores in Italy and Switzerland. In 2000, he opened his first chocolate store. Today, he has cafés all over the world, which are popular for coffee and for the thirty different flavors of homemade ice cream you can buy. His smooth, creamy ice cream is made from fresh milk, cocoa from Venezuela, Colombian coffee, and nuts from Italy. No one knows how Vecchia makes it. That's a secret!

In 2011, Vecchia organized the World Chocolate Exhibition. He visited many famous sites around the world, from Egyptian temples to places in Europe. Then, together with other artists, Vecchia carefully built a miniature of each place he visited in white chocolate. White chocolate is extremely difficult to work with. The sugar, cocoa butter, and milk solids must be exactly the right temperature. Despite this, in July 2012 Vecchia successfully made the largest chocolate sculpture in the world! It is more than 4 meters tall and took one month to freeze! The question is: How does he make the sculptures without eating them? Amazing!

Mexican painter and sculptor Elena Climent made a whole room of chocolate! Using 420 kilograms of dark, milk, and white chocolate, she made chocolate sofas, tables, carpets, paintings, and spoons! Eventually, the room was broken into pieces, and the chocolate was given to visitors.

24 **Read and circle.** Answer the questions.

1. A chocolatier is someone who makes . . .
   a. dishes from chocolate b. large chocolate sculptures
2. The . . . for Vecchia's ice cream is a secret.
   a. origin b. recipe
3. His chocolate sculptures of ancient sites are . . .
   a. the same size as the original places b. smaller than the real sites
4. It is difficult to carve white chocolate because it . . .
   a. must not be too hot or too cold b. contains sugar and cocoa butter

25 **Read the text again.** Complete the timeline.

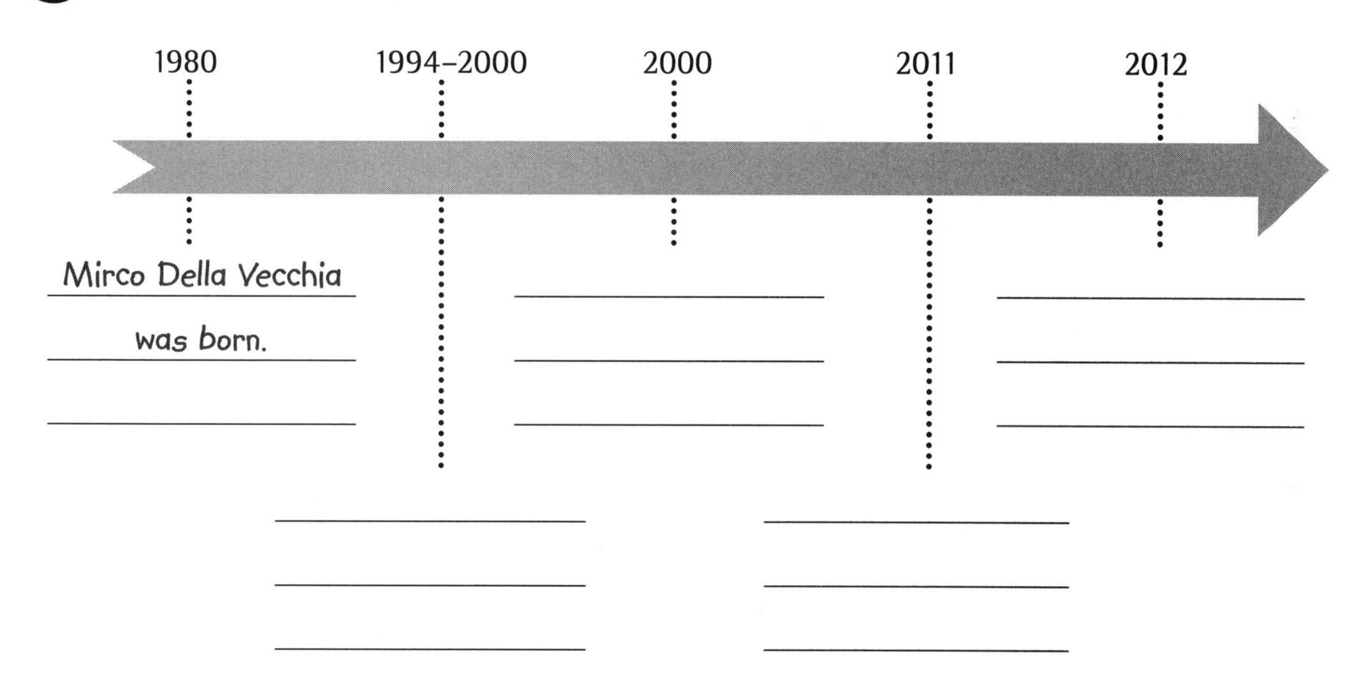

26 **Write your opinion in your notebook.**

1. What's the most interesting thing about Vecchia?
2. What is the coolest thing he has done?
3. What is the best thing about his chocolate?
4. Can we really call chocolate sculptures a kind of art?

27 **Do a role play.** Interview your partner. Then change roles.

1. You are Mirco Della Vecchia. Answer your partner's questions.
2. You want to write a blog about Vecchia. Ask your partner some questions.

28 Read *Chocolate Customs* on page 48 of your Student Book.

How did the writers plan their writing? Read the steps.

1. First, the writers chose a special occasion in their country when people use chocolate.

   Japan: Valentine's Day

   Mexico: Day of the Dead

2. Next, the writers wrote down *main ideas* about the celebrations. They used word maps.

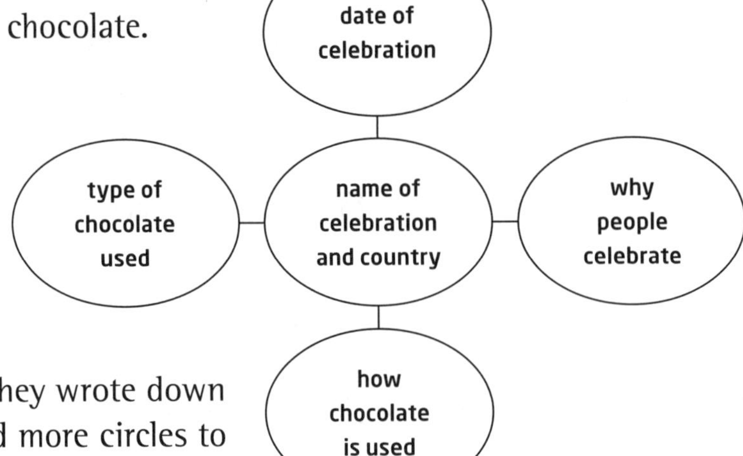

3. After writing the main ideas, they wrote down supporting details. They added more circles to the word map to do this.

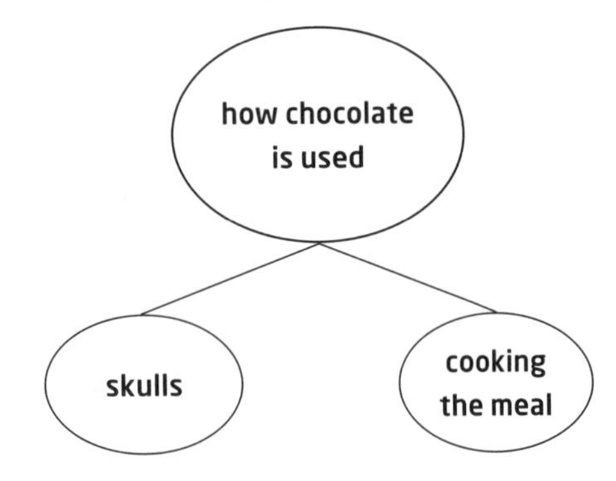

4. Next, they checked that there was "unity" and made changes if necessary.

   Are the supporting details next to the relevant main idea?

   Is there any information that doesn't belong?

5. Then, they numbered the order in which they wanted to write the main ideas.

   (1) the name of the celebration

   (2) why people celebrate it

   (3) the dates - and what happens on those dates

Read the Mexico paragraph. Number the order of the main ideas.

(____) why people celebrate it

(__1__) the name of the celebration and the date

(____) how we use chocolate

6. Finally, they wrote their first version, called a draft, of the paragraph.

   Now it's time to plan your own writing.

29 **Now follow steps 1-6 on page 36.** Write your paragraph about a chocolate custom in your notebook. Check your paragraph for unity before you share it with your teacher or with other students.

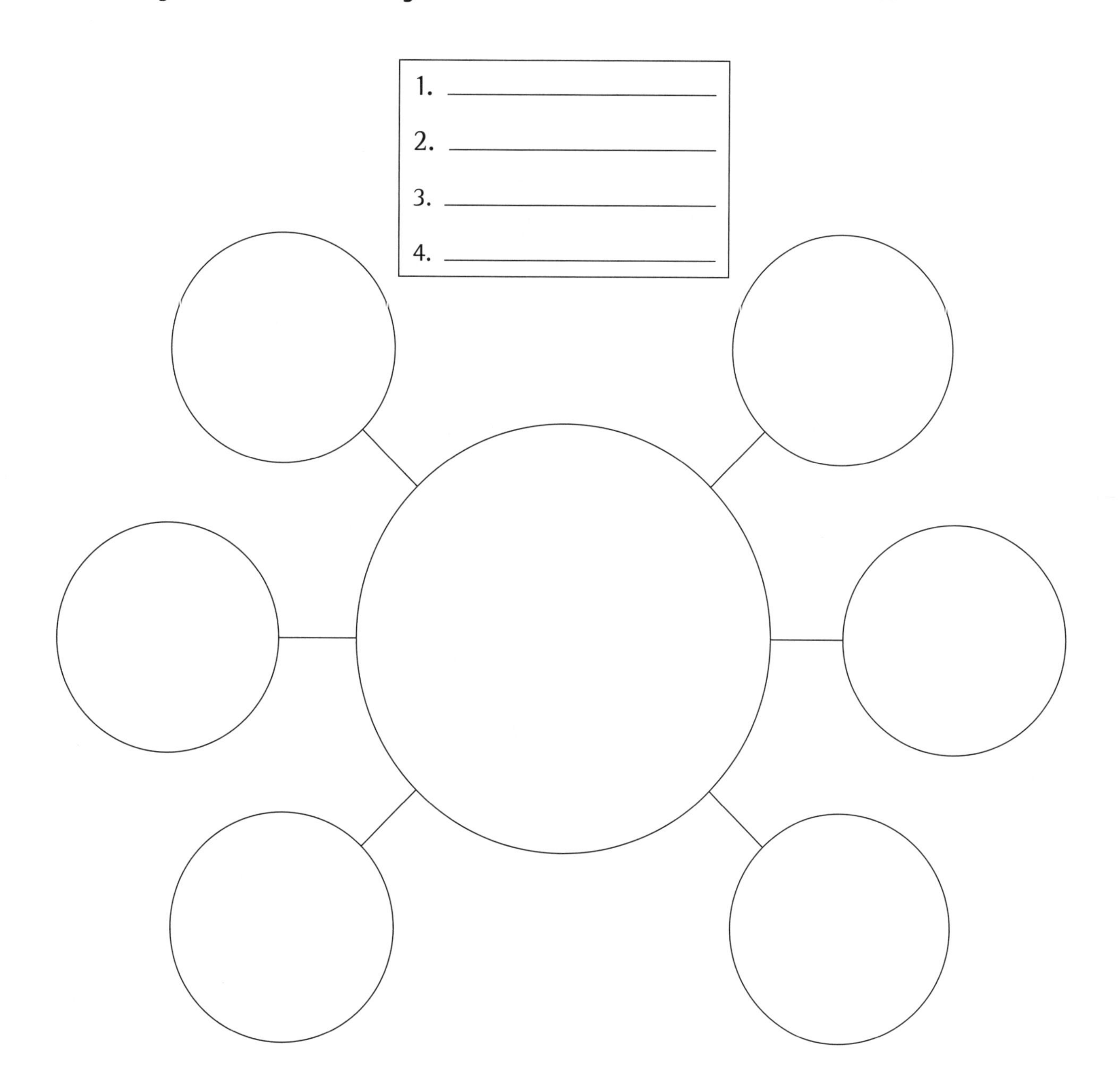

30 **Express yourself.** Choose one of the topics below and write a unified paragraph. Plan your writing and follow the steps on page 36. Write your new paragraph in your notebook.

What is a custom in your country that you like?

What are cafés and cake shops like in your country?

Review

1 **Read.** Underline the word that does not belong.

1. hot chocolate	recipe	ice cream	milk shake
2. DNA test	CT scan	sample	solid
3. elbow pads	helmets	injuries	knee pads
4. cinnamon	vanilla	cocoa powder	artifacts
5. archaeologists	thieves	tattoos	rulers
6. mummies	cause	statues	treasure

2 **Read and write.** Explain the reason why each word you underlined in Activity 1 does not belong. Use the clues below to help you.

archaeologists equipment ~~food and drink~~ ingredients objects at sites people

accident ~~cook~~ liquid objects paint reason

1. Hot chocolate, ice cream, and milk shakes are kinds of food and drink. Recipes tell us how to cook food and drink.

2. ______________________________

3. ______________________________

4. ______________________________

5. ______________________________

6. ______________________________

3 **Listen.** Underline the correct answers. **TR: 21**

1. Mario is surprised by the *height* / *length* / *origin* of the statues.
2. Qin Shi Huang *was born* / *became ruler* / *was buried* in 246 BCE.
3. The ruler died *just before* / *when* / *soon after* the men finished the work.
4. Some farmers discovered *tombs* / *artifacts* / *statues* in 1974.

4 **Read and write.** Finish the questions. Then answer them.

1. What ___was___ the ruler ___thinking___ (think) about when he was 13?

   He ___was planning___ (plan) his next life.

2. What ____________ Mario ____________ (do) when he was 13?

   He ____________ (study) in school.

3. Why ____________ men ____________ (make) statues for 36 years?

   They ____________ (build) an army for their ruler.

4. How long ____________ the archaeologists ____________ (work) on the site?

   They ____________ (excavate) it for twenty years.

5 **Write.** Make true sentences.

1. statues / build / thousands of men

   The statues were built by thousands of men.

2. ruler / bury / 210 BCE

   ____

3. some artifacts / find / farmers

   ____

4. site / excavate / archaeologists

   ____

6 **Read and write.** Write what each person did to help the chocolate reach you.

You have just bought some chocolate from a store. Your chocolate came from a tree near the equator, but how did it reach you? Who did the work? When the tree was about five meters tall, farmers picked the cocoa pods. They cut them open and took out the beans. Before the farmers put the beans in sacks to sell them, they had to leave them in the shade for a week and then dry them in the sun for ten days. After that, someone took the farmers' sacks to a port by truck and sent them to a factory by plane or ship. Ingredients were then added, and the chocolate was put into a mold. Finally, the candy was wrapped and packed. Can you guess what happened next?

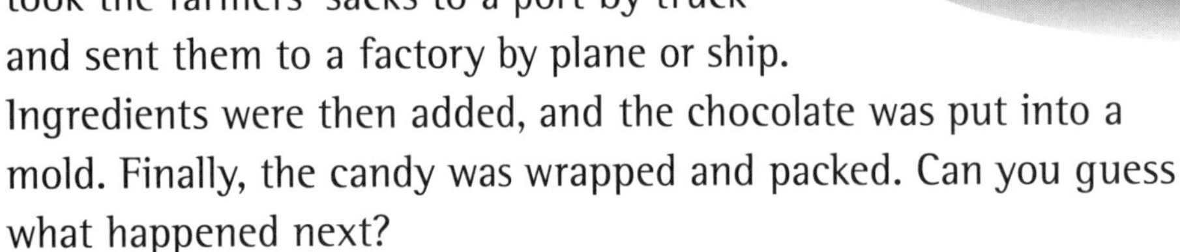

1. A shop assistant sold me the candy bar in the store.
2. Farmers ______________________ the pods.
3. Farmers ______________________ the beans.
4. A truck driver ______________________.
5. Factory workers ______________________.

7 **Match the questions and answers.**

1. What's this recipe for?
2. Sure. What ingredients do we need?
3. How much cocoa powder should I add?
4. The ingredients are here. What next?
5. Where do I pour the liquid?

a. Mix them together for one minute.
b. Put it into these two glasses.
c. Vanilla ice cream, milk, cocoa powder, sugar, and bananas.
d. Banana milk shakes. Let's make them now!
e. Six grams. Add a teaspoon of sugar, too.

8 **Read and write.** Complete the paragraph. There are some extra words.

accident brakes equipment hang-gliding injuries land
life jackets ~~really~~ skillfully strength totally

I've been at Sports Camp for four days, and it's ___really___ great! Our teachers are wonderful, and we use really modern __________ (even our surf-boards are new)! We wear yellow __________, which don't look very cool, but they're important if we have an __________. My surfing is better than it was last year, but I'm still not very strong. I need more __________ in my legs. Some of the girls can surf really __________. Why don't you come next year? We could learn motocross, or a sport like __________.

9 **Write.**

1. Imagine you are at a sports camp. What two things have you learned to do?

____

____

2. Have you made any new friends? Have you eaten anything new? Have you slept in a tent?

____

____

3. What is the best thing you have done since you've been there?

____

____

Unit 4

Water, Water Everywhere!

1 **Find and circle the words in the puzzle.**

A	C	C	S	O	A	K	W	F	R	F
S	W	A	M	P	D	X	F	L	V	I
O	B	T	R	Y	H	A	R	O	Z	L
H	Q	Z	I	V	M	R	E	A	J	T
G	L	A	C	I	E	R	E	T	O	E
B	A	W	N	T	C	I	Z	O	M	R
P	K	A	W	F	S	Q	E	C	L	K
A	E	N	E	M	J	T	K	L	U	P
S	A	L	T	W	A	T	E	R	K	S
P	O	Y	I	N	R	V	Y	C	S	X
A	J	W	A	T	E	R	F	A	L	L

~~carve~~	saltwater
filter	sea
float	soak
freeze	swamp
glacier	waterfall
lake	wet

2 **Look and write.** Label the pictures.

carve

______

______

______

______

3 **Write and listen.** Complete the description. Then listen to check your answers. TR: 22

carved	~~float~~	freeze	freshwater
glaciers	lakes	sea	sea level

The awesome Huangshan Mountains of China seem to float on top of the clouds! They were __________ by __________ about 100 million years ago when an ancient __________ disappeared. Today, the area is famous for beautiful rocks, clear blue __________, and waterfalls. It's also popular for its food, especially the delicious __________ crabs. If you plan on visiting, take warm clothes in winter so you don't __________ at night (you are 1,800 meters above __________), and don't forget to take your camera for those amazing views!

4 **Listen.** Complete the chart. TR: 23

	Country	Bodies of Water	Interesting Fact
Easter Island	Chile	three freshwater lakes	There are 800 stone statues, and no one knows who carved them.
Iguazu Falls			
Huascaran National Park			

5 Label the pictures.

a puddle of water   a tall glass of water   water for crops   water for plants

________ ________ ________ ________

6 **Listen.** Complete the lines in the song. TR: 24

A puddle of water.	We need ________
A waterfall.	and water for grass.
________.	We need ________ and
I love it all!	animals, too!

7 **Listen.** What has the singer been thinking about? Check **T** for *True* and **F** for *False*. TR: 25

1. There are many types of water in the world. (T) (F)
2. Nothing needs water. (T) (F)
3. We need water for many things in this world. (T) (F)

8 **Work with a partner.** Write a new chorus.

There's water ________,
and water ________.
There's even water
________!
________, ________, water ________.
It's everywhere!

GRAMMAR

I You We They	**have (not) been**	taking time to think. drinking hot cocoa. swimming. kitesurfing.	**have been = 've been**
He/She/It	**has (not) been**		**has been = 's been**

How long Where Why	**have**	I you we they	**been**	swimming?	Have you been . . . ? Yes, I have. / No, I haven't.
	has	he/she/it			

9 **Write.** Write what these people have been doing.

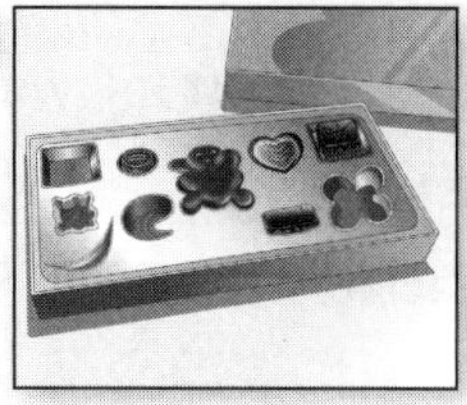

eat   excavate   sit   ~~swim~~   watch

1. The girl's hair is wet. She's been swimming in the lake.
2. The archaeologist is tired, and his back hurts. ______________ a site since this morning.
3. The woman has a sunburn. ______________ in the sun for hours.
4. The boys don't want any dinner now! ______________ candy all afternoon.
5. The kids are feeling really happy. ______________ dolphins for nearly an hour.

10 **Read and write.** Complete the sentences.

drain faucet leak save

1. What happened? Why is your hand all blue? Has your pen been ________ again?
2. I'm so happy. I've been ________ money for months, and now I have enough!
3. Did you know that some ________ go directly to lakes and rivers?
4. Why should we turn off the ________ when we brush our teeth?

11 **Read.** Match the items in Activity 10 with these items.

☐ a. Congratulations! What are you going to buy?

☐ b. Oh no. I also have ink on my shirt! I need to soak it in some water.

☐ c. No way! That means our garbage kills freshwater fish. That's really bad.

☐ d. Because it's a great way to save water.

12 **Listen.** Complete the chart. TR: 26

	How did these people waste water in the past?	How do they save water now?
1.	She used to take baths.	Now she takes showers.
2.	He used to leave the water running when he brushed his teeth.	________________
3.	________________ ________________	She has painted fish on the drains to help her remember.
4.	He used to have old faucets in his home.	________________ ________________

13 **Write.** In your notebook, describe some of the ideas you heard about in Activity 12. Which was the most useful? Which is the easiest to change? Who made the biggest difference?

14 Look and write.

a glacier   a lake   a sea   a swamp   a waterfall

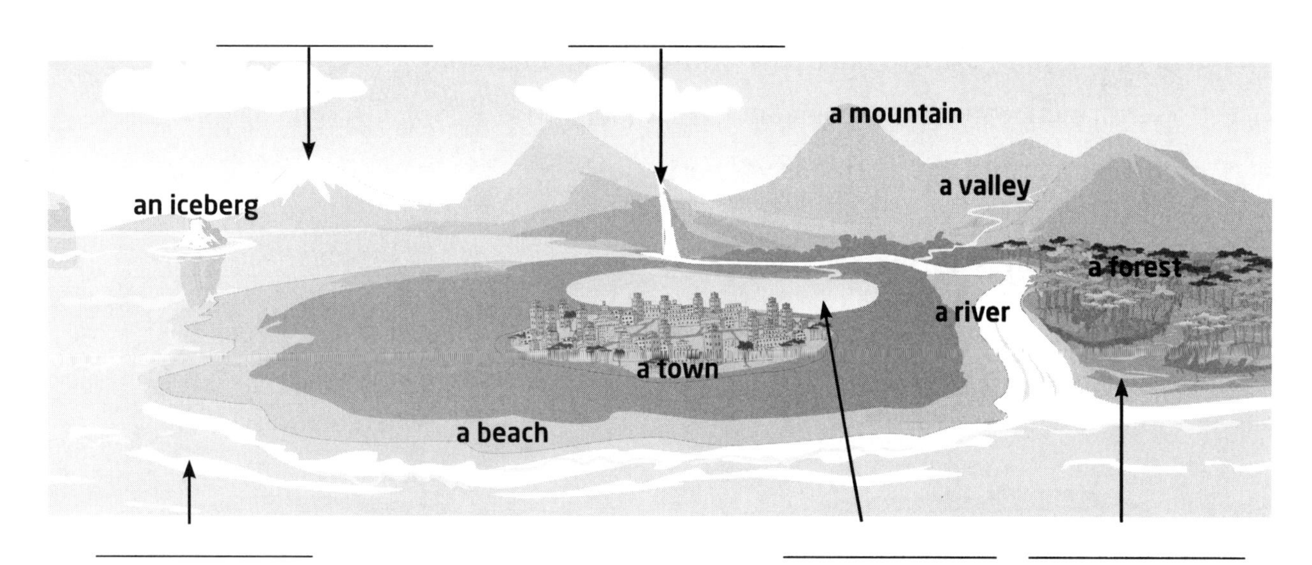

______ ______ ______

15 **Look and read.** Look at the picture in Activity 14. Check **T** for *True* or **F** for *False*.

1. There is a glacier at the top of the mountain. (T) ✓ (F)
2. An iceberg is floating in the lake. (T) (F)
3. The town is below sea level. (T) (F)
4. Next to the waterfall is a swamp. (T) (F)
5. The swamp is almost at sea level. (T) (F)
6. A river has carved through the valley on its way to the sea. (T) (F)

16 **Listen.** Complete the sentences. **TR: 27**

1. a. Rivers begin their journey in a high place above sea level.
   b. The source of a river can be a glacier or a ______ lake.
   c. Millions of ______ of rain join the river on its journey to the sea.
2. a. At the mouth, the river empties into the sea and mixes with ______.
   b. Some rivers empty into a bigger river or ______.
   c. Sometimes a river doesn't reach the sea. It ends in a ______.
3. a. The people in the town probably get their ______ from the lake.
   b. Fresh water travels from the lake to their ______.
   c. The dirty water that goes down people's ______ goes into water below the town.

GRAMMAR

Whenever I swim in the lake, I feel really good.

I feel really good **whenever** I swim in the lake.

Wherever you go, there are people without running water.

Do **whatever** you can to save water. It's important.

Whoever painted this picture is very artistic.

17 Match the conversations.

1. Can I please bring a friend to the party?
2. Would you like vanilla or chocolate cake?
3. Where do you want to go?
4. What time should I call you tomorrow?

a. I don't mind. **Wherever** you like!

b. Sure! **Whoever** wants to come is welcome!

c. **Whenever** you can. I'll be home all day.

d. I'll have **whatever** you have.

18 Read and write. Complete the sentences.

1. I love Brazil. __________ you go, you meet nice people.
2. Come around and see me ________ you like. It's always good to see you!
3. ________ told you that showers waste more water than baths is wrong.
4. _________ she tried to do, she failed. However, she always tried again until she succeeded!

19 **Write.** Write questions. Then look at the pictures and write the answers.

1a. What / the children / do?

What have the children been doing? They've been playing in the water.

1b. They / save / water?

Have they been saving water?

2a. How long / Lisa / sleep?

____

2b. Study / recently?

____

20 **Listen and write.** Listen to the conversations. Complete the sentences. **TR: 28**

1. Well, ____________, stop it right now. You're wasting water.
2. That's true, but you can't sleep ____________. You missed Grandma!

21 **Write about your home life in your notebook.** What do you have to do? What can and can't you do?

call my parents	have a party
eat sweets and treats	sleep
friends	spend money

whenever
whatever
wherever
whoever

22 **Listen and read.** TR: 29

Water Cycle Wonders

When you drink a glass of fresh water, your water is very old! In fact, the same water has been traveling around Earth since before King Tut. The water cycle is the process of how water moves around the planet. There are four main phases. In each phase, water can be liquid, solid (ice), or gas (vapor). Let's learn more!

Evaporation: When the sun heats Earth's surface water, that water becomes water vapor or steam. The vapor rises into the air and changes from liquid to gas. Evaporation can take place at any temperature.

Condensation: Some vapor comes back down to us as rain. How does vapor become liquid? It condenses! As evaporated water rises into the atmosphere, it becomes cold and forms water droplets. Millions of droplets then form clouds.

Precipitation: When clouds become heavy with condensed water, the atmosphere can no longer hold the water. It then falls back to Earth in the form of rain, snow, or ice, depending on the temperature.

Collection: When precipitation lands on Earth, it moves in different ways. Some water moves across the land (*runoff*), but some water soaks into the earth (*infiltration*) and moves underground. Water collects in many places—even glaciers—and eventually evaporates again. Wherever it lands, water keeps moving!

23 **Read and look.** Label the four photos.

1. 

precipitation
____

2. 

____

3. 

____

4. 

____

24 Read and write.

gas liquid(s) solid(s)

1. Water vapor is a kind of ___gas___. As it rises, it gets colder.
2. Frozen water on glaciers and ice are two kinds of ________.
3. Groundwater and runoff is ________ water.
4. Evaporation is the process during which liquid water changes to a ________.
5. Condensation is the process during which a gas changes to a ________.
6. Precipitation is the process during which water returns to Earth as a ________ or a liquid.

25 **Work with a partner.** Explain the four stages of the water cycle. Use the diagram to help you.

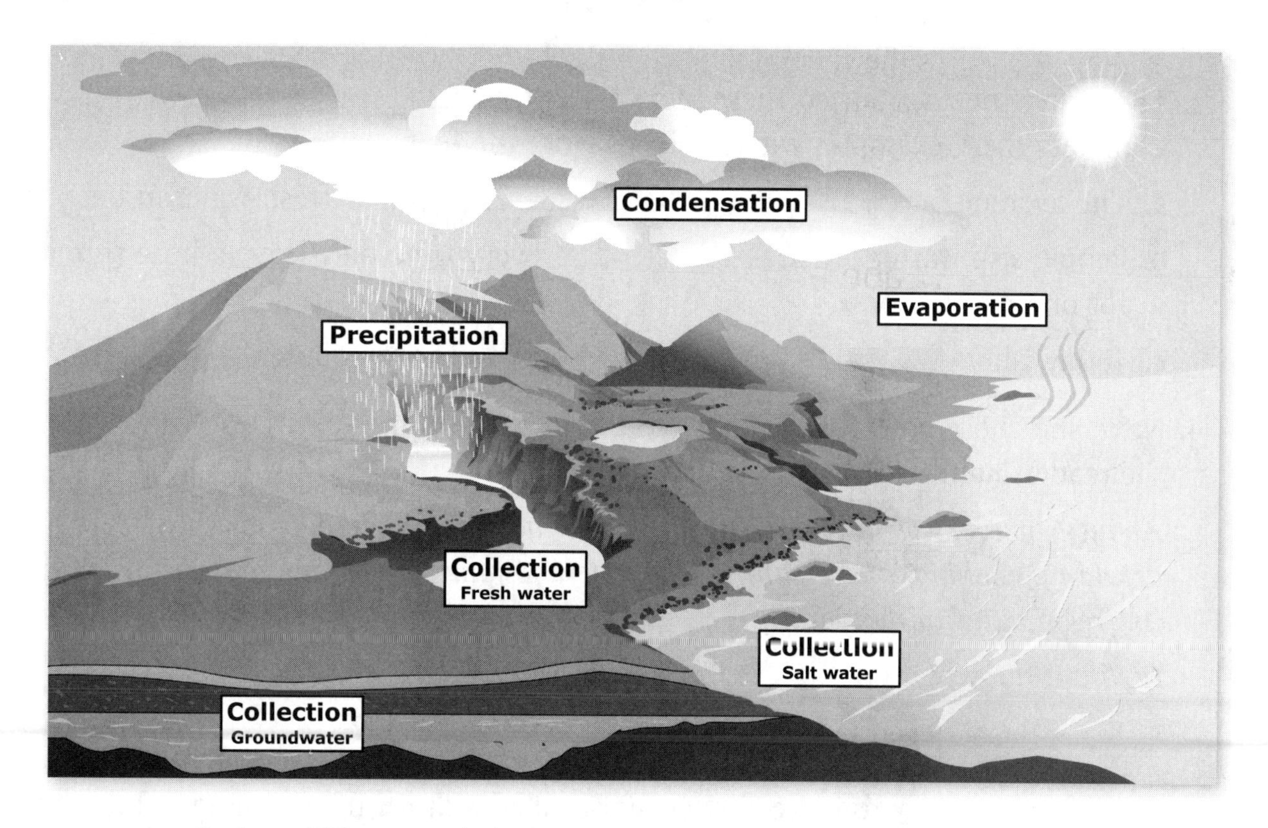

During a 100-year period, an average water molecule spends 98 years in the ocean, 20 months as ice, about 2 weeks in lakes and rivers, and less than a week in the air.

26 **Read *Save Water Outdoors!* on page 68 of your Student Book.** How did the writer plan her writing? Read the steps.

1. First, the writer chose a topic and did some research on ways to save water outdoors: *How do people waste water in the yard? What could we do instead?* She then made some notes.
2. After reading about how people waste water outdoors, the writer wrote down some ideas. Next, she organized her notes in a T-chart. Complete the chart.

How do we waste/pollute water?	How could we save water?
We water plants when it's hot.	Water plants before 9 a.m.
____________________	Turn them off!
____________________	Use rainwater.
____________________	Don't wash cars at home.

3. The writer then supported these ideas with statistics. Complete these examples with statistics from the text.
   a. The average family uses ____________ of their fresh water in the yard!
   b. People also waste ____________ every time they leave a hose running for one minute.
   c. Today, about ____________ of our rivers are polluted.
4. Next, she chose powerful statistics to begin and end the text. This makes the reader interested in her writing.

   About 5 percent of the world's fresh water goes to our homes for drinking, cooking, and cleaning. The average family uses one quarter of its fresh water in the yard!

   How did the writer end her text? ____________________

   ____
5. Finally, the writer wrote the first version, called a draft, of her paragraph. Now it's time to plan your own writing.

27 **What do you remember about wasting and saving water indoors?** Write information in the box below. Look through Unit 4 in your Student Book if you need help. Note facts and statistics that will help you as you plan your writing.

Facts and Statistics

28 **Now follow steps 2-5 on page 52.** Use the T-chart to organize your notes. Write your paragraph on ways to "save water indoors" in your notebook.

29 **Express yourself.** Choose one of the topics below. Plan your writing, and follow the steps on page 52. Include facts and statistics. Write your new paragraph in your notebook.

- a famous river, lake, or waterfall
- a place with water that you recommend to visitors
- interesting facts about your hometown
- interesting facts about a country you would like to visit

Unit 5

It's a Small World

1 **Read and write.** Do the puzzle. Find the secret message.

Scrambled word	Boxes	Numbered boxes
CLLE	c e l l	13
MIEREMLITL	10 boxes	2, 17
TMTEERICNE	10 boxes	10
TAITAHB	7 boxes	9
CEURETRA	8 boxes	6
BRGA	4 boxes	12
RLCAW	5 boxes	15, 4
MOMNCO	6 boxes	18, 19, 20
GONRIASM	8 boxes	7, 14
MAUNH	5 boxes	11
LEAM	4 boxes	5
FMLEAE	6 boxes	3, 21
NITH	4 boxes	
CIPCESMORO	10 boxes	16, 1
ROIHBREL	8 boxes	8

~~cell~~
centimeter
common
crawl
creature
female
grab
habitat
horrible
human
male
microscope
millimeter
organism
thin

1 2 3 4 5   6 7 8 9 10 11 12 13 14   15 16 17   18 19 20 21 !

2 **Read and write.** Complete the paragraph.

cell   creatures   habitats   microscope   millimeters

Have you ever seen an amoeba? They're awesome __________! They only have one __________. You can find them in lots of different __________, especially in fresh water. Amoebas are really small. The biggest ones are only about eight __________ in length. Some are much smaller than that, so you have to look at them through a __________.

3 **Listen and write.** Answer the questions. **TR: 30**

1. Why is it amazing to watch amoebas through a microscope?

   ____

2. What can these funny organisms do?

   ____

3. Are amoebas male, female, or both?

   ____

4 **Write.** Complete the sentences.

1. I think the most amazing thing about amoebas is ____________________

   ____________________.

2. The worst thing about amoebas is ____________________.

3. In my opinion, amoebas are ____________________ creatures because

   ____________________.

5 **Work with a partner.** Compare your opinions about amoebas. How similar and different are your opinions?

6 **Listen and read.** Listen to the words that rhyme in each column. **TR: 31**

1	2	3	4	5	6
features	where	jaws	dies	their	day
creatures	care	laws	size	there	hey
teachers	hair	claws	eyes	bear	prey

7 **Listen and write.** Choose the best word from each column and write it in the song. **TR: 32**

My teacher said that ___creatures___
smaller than a human ________
live in our world.
She said we'd find them everywhere!

Some look like strange monsters,
with jaws and ________ and horrible eyes.
But don't forget how small they are.
Don't forget their ________.

________ are tiny habitats
where predator and ________
have tiny little battles
every minute of the day.

8 **Write.** Write another verse to the song. Imagine that you are a very small creature. Describe humans from your point of view.

My teacher said that ___humans___ live in our world.

She said we'd find people everywhere!

Some people look like ________________________.

And other people ________________________.

There are enormous habitats where humans ________________

____

____.

GRAMMAR

Teacher: "It **is** a small world. There **are** creatures everywhere."

My teacher said it **was** a small world. She said there **were** creatures everywhere.

Teacher: "Tiny creatures **live** in our world, but we **don't see** them all."

My teacher said that tiny creatures **lived** in our world, but we **didn't see** them all.

Teacher: "**You can** find them everywhere! **You will** find them if you look."

She said (that) **we could** find them everywhere! She told us that **we would** find them if we **looked**.

9 **Read and write.** What did the tour guide say? Report the information.

1. An octopus has three hearts.
2. A giraffe is as tall as nine koala bears.
3. Some fish can walk on land.
4. Hummingbirds can't smell.
5. The seahorse grabs food with its tail.

What did the tour guide say?

1. He said that an octopus had three hearts.
2. ______________________
3. ______________________
4. ______________________
5. ______________________

10 **Listen and read.** Underline the correct words. **TR: 33**

1. She said that *my* / *her* / *his* name was Mrs. Li.
2. She told us that *I* / *he* / *she* was our new science teacher.
3. She said that *we* / *you* / *they* were going to learn many interesting things.
4. She told *us* / *them* / *you* that we would work hard.
5. She said that we would enjoy learning with *me* / *him* / *her*.

11 **Look and write.** Label the pictures.

adult furry pointed spotted strange tiny

strange

12 Read and match.

1. d What can we buy Mom for her birthday? She wants something fun and colorful.
2. ____ Mrs. Li, why do we need to use a microscope to see mites?
3. ____ Can you see that strange thing in the trees? What is it?
4. ____ Little children shouldn't use scissors. They're dangerous.
5. ____ Why do you have so many stuffed toys?
6. ____ Your brother is amazing. He's only ten years old, but he isn't like other kids.

a. I don't know, but I'm scared. Let's run!

b. They're cute and furry! Look at this teddy bear, for example.

c. I agree. Sharp, pointed things can cause serious accidents.

d. How about a spotted umbrella? This one has pretty red spots.

e. I know. He likes to play chess, watch the news, and read adult books.

f. They're tiny. You can't see them with your eyes.

13 **Read.** Underline the correct words in the paragraph.

The pygmy marmoset is the smallest monkey in the world. It is ***big* / *tiny***. A baby pygmy marmoset is only 25 mm long—as long as a ***human's* / *creature's*** finger! Adults are bigger and have a body length of 14 to 16 ***millimeters* / *centimeters***. The males are heavier than females (males weigh around 140 grams, but ***males* / *females*** only weigh 120 grams). The ***baby* / *adult*** male takes care of the young, carrying the babies around on his back until they are about two months old. Pygmy marmosets, whose natural ***habitat* / *microscope*** is the Amazon rainforest, are cute. They have sharp ***pointed* / *common*** teeth and claws, so they can eat from trees. These strong ***cells* / *creatures*** can move extremely quickly through the trees.

14 **Look and listen.** Listen to the story. Answer the questions. **TR: 34**

1. What does Mrs. Gonzalez look like?

   She's tall and thin, with a big smile.

2. What happened to Mrs. Gonzalez's bag?

   ____

3. Who was the thief that grabbed Mrs. Gonzalez's bag?

   ____

4. What does the boy say about monkeys stealing food?

   ____

5. What was the monkey doing when the police found it?

   ____

15 **Work with a partner.** Discuss the questions.

1. Why do humans put animals in zoos?
2. What is good and bad about zoos?
3. What are the two most common creatures you see every day?
4. Which creature would you most like to see? What habitat does it live in?

GRAMMAR

opinion	size	age	shape	color	pattern	origin	material	thing
cute	long	young	round	red	striped	Chinese	furry	ears
amazing	tiny	old	wide	blue	spotted	Spanish	hairy	tails
horrible	tall	ancient	pointed	gray		Brazilian	plastic	wings
ugly	short	adult	straight	green		Japanese	silver	bugs
cool	little	baby	thin	black		French	metal	

a **cute little green Colombian** frog

two **pretty red spotted** flowers

amazing long pointed tails

horrible black furry spiders

16 **Read, write, and listen.** Write the adjectives in the correct order. Then listen to check your answers. **TR: 35**

1. Marmosets have cute brown furry bodies. (*brown / furry / cute*)
2. Hey, I like these ________ insects. (*striped / Australian / cool*)
3. Oh, look at these ________ frogs! (*green / tiny / amazing*)
4. Mites are ________ organisms. (*ugly / gray / round*)
5. The Arctic hare has ________ ears. (*white / furry / soft*)

17 **Read and write.** Write descriptions. Use two to three adjectives each time.

1. You're an archaeologist. You've found something very interesting. Describe it.

   I've found a wonderful ancient stone statue.

2. You want to go swimming in the lake today. What's the weather like?

   It's ________ day.

3. It's incredibly hot today. You'd like an ice cream. What do you order?

   Excuse me, I'd like a(n) ________, please!

4. You are walking through a forest and suddenly you see a butterfly. Describe it.

   It has ________.

18 **Read and write.** Report what these people/creatures said.

Male friend: "Seahorses are a kind of horse." Me: "You're crazy! They live in the ocean and are fish!"

1. My friend told ___me___ that ___seahorses were a kind of horse___.
2. I told ______ that he ______.
3. I said that they ______ and ______.

Male bug: "I can't sleep. Humans make a lot of noise!" Female bug: "I agree. They shout all the time."

4. The male bug said that ______.
5. He said that humans ______.
6. The female bug said that ______ and that they ______.

19 **Read and write.** Write what the tour guide said.

1. Our guide said that these awesome adult frogs ___changed___ (change) color when they ______ (feel) scared.
2. She said that the common little red bug ______ (have) a spotted back so that predators ______ (will) think its spots ______ (be) poisonous.
3. She said that the Denise seahorse ______ (be) a strange orange color so other creatures ______ (not / can) see it when it ______ (move) in the orange coral.

20 **Work with a partner.** Student 1, go to page 123. Student 2, go to page 125. Take turns.

21 **Write.** What do you know about spiders? What would you like to know? Complete Columns 1 and 2 of the chart.

I know	I would like to know	I learned

 **Listen and read.** TR: 36

Web Masters

A hairy tarantula crawls along a branch. He is one of 40,000 different spiders that live on Earth. Spiders live in many habitats, from rain forests to deserts, but they don't live in oceans. There are probably some in your home, too! You can find spiders in many sizes. A goliath tarantula is bigger than your hand, whereas the tiny *patua* spider is less than a millimeter long. A few spiders poison people, but don't be scared. It isn't common! In fact, spiders *help* humans because they eat insects—and mice—which destroy our crops. These wonderful web masters help balance life on Earth.

Spiders are wonderful but strange creatures. Most can't see clearly, so they have up to eight eyes to help them find their dinner! They are similar to insects in many ways, but they are in fact arachnids. They have two body parts, no wings, and eight legs (whereas insects have three body parts, up to four wings, and six legs). Using spinnerets, spiders make silk and spin strong webs. Once the prey is in the web, it's time to eat. The spider's mouth is awesome. The palps, next to its jaws, are like arms. They hold the prey still. Then the strong fangs bite. Ouch!

23 **Work with a partner.** Refer to the chart in Activity 21.

1. Reread the questions you wrote in Column 2. Does the text tell you what you would like to know?
2. What interesting things did you learn about spiders? Make notes in Column 3.

Spider silk is one of the strongest materials on Earth. Some spiders can make silk that is stronger than steel!

24 **Read and write.** Check **T** for *True* or **F** for *False*.

1. You can find spiders in all habitats. (T) (F)
2. Spiders rarely attack or hurt people. (T) (F)
3. Spiders do an important job on our planet. (T) (F)
4. The spider's prey can't escape because of its fangs. (T) (F)

25 **Look and read.** Label the picture.

eyes fang legs palp spider's web spinneret

26 **Work with a partner.** Talk about spiders. How are they different from—and similar to—insects?

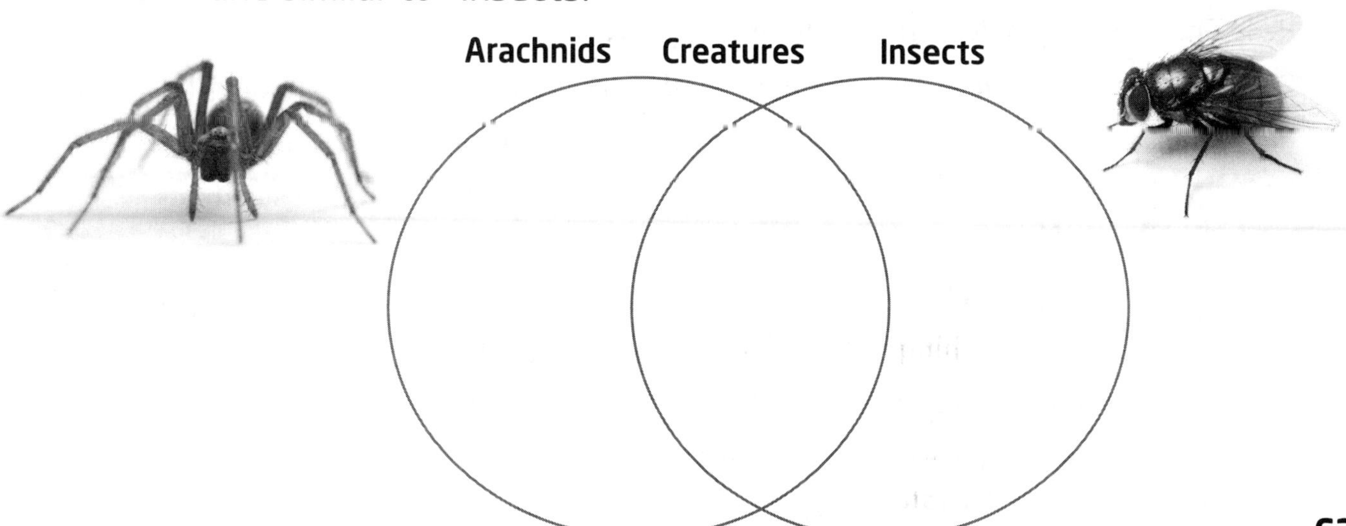

27 **Read *An Interesting Sea Creature* on page 84 of your Student Book.** How did the writer plan her writing? Read the steps.

1. First, the writer chose a creature to review: ______________________________.
2. Next, the writer wrote down a list of details she could write about. She used an ideas map.

scientific information	habitat	food	physical characteristics	interesting facts
• *Hippocampus denise* • species of fish • discovered by Australian biologist Rudie Kulter	• coral reefs • Asia • found at a depth of 13-90 meters below sea level	• soft coral	• light orange color • long thin pointed tail • total length of 16 millimeters (about 0.6 inches)	• males have babies • can carry 10-1,000 babies

3. Next, she researched the creature and completed the chart with statistics and details.
4. Then she organized the paragraphs by topic.

   Read her paragraphs, and write which details she included in each paragraph.

   Paragraph 1: scientific/common names; type of species; habitat; ____________

   Paragraph 2: ______________________; some information from a scientist

   Paragraph 3: ______________________; conclusion
5. Finally, she wrote the first version, called a draft, of her paragraph. She used facts, statistics, and lots of descriptions to explain the size, shape, color, pattern, and origin of the creature. For example: *long pointed tail.*

   Now it's time to plan your own writing.

28 **Follow steps 1-5 on page 64.** Use this idea map to organize your notes. Write your animal report in your notebook.

29 **Express yourself.** Choose one of the topics below to write a report about. Include facts, statistics, and descriptions. End with a conclusion. Plan your writing and follow the steps on page 64. Write your new report in your notebook.

A tree, flower, or plant
Something in space
Something you learned about in a science class

Unit 6

Smart Choices

1 Label the pictures.

~~break~~ cost dip drop fix test

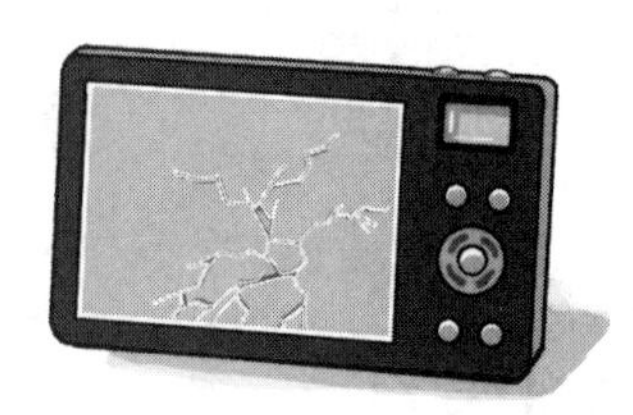

break

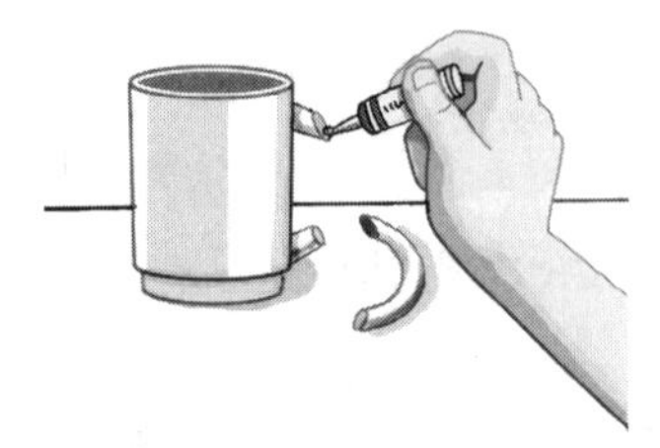

2 **Listen.** Choose the correct answer. TR: 37

1. Mom bought a new pair of glasses. What happened?
   a. They were made of glass. One day, she dropped them and they broke.
   b. They were made of a material that doesn't break, but they broke on impact.
2. Dad bought some waterproof boots. What happened to them?
   a. While he was fishing in the river, they filled with water.
   b. To test them, he dipped them in the river. They got wet.
3. I bought a new T-shirt, and it cost a lot of money. What happened?
   a. While I was playing soccer, it tore.
   b. When I soaked it in water, it changed color.

3 Do the puzzle.

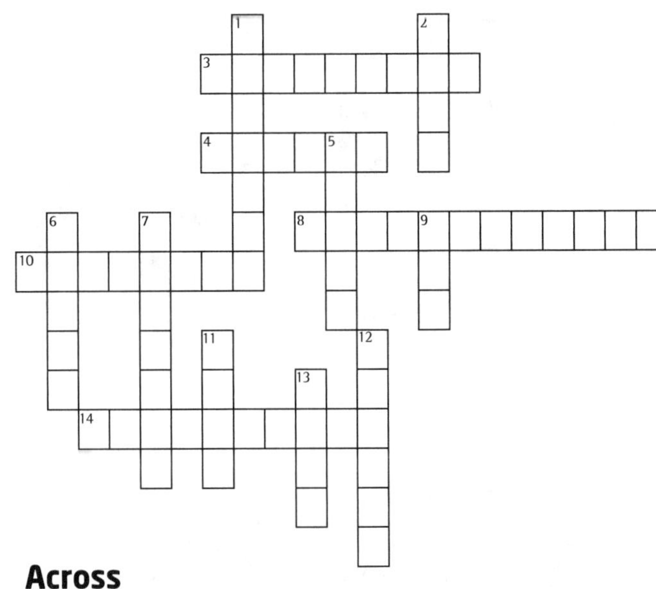

break	impact
cost	manufacturer
crash	products
customers	quality
drop	safety
dummies	torn
fix	waterproof

Across

3. People who buy things
4. It broke on _____.
8. A company that makes something
10. Things that people buy
14. Something that water can't enter

Down

1. Statues that look like people
2. It's made of glass. Don't _____ it!
5. Every year, many cars are sent for _____ tests.
6. How did you _____ your camera?
7. This is cheap, but it's good _____!
9. It's broken. Can you please _____ it?
11. I fell off my bike. My pants got _____.
12. Life jackets are important for this.
13. How much does it _____?

4 **What about your friends and family?** Answer the questions. Then describe what happened in your notebook.

Have your friends or relatives ever bought a product that

a. broke when they got home? 

b. tore? 

c. was supposed to be waterproof but wasn't? 

d. they dropped? yes no

e. cost a lot of money but didn't work? yes 

f. the manufacturer fixed for them? yes no

5 **Read and listen.** Check the words you hear in the song. **TR: 38**

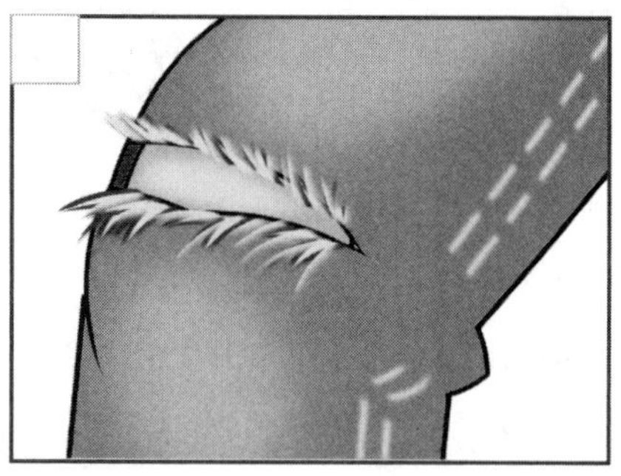

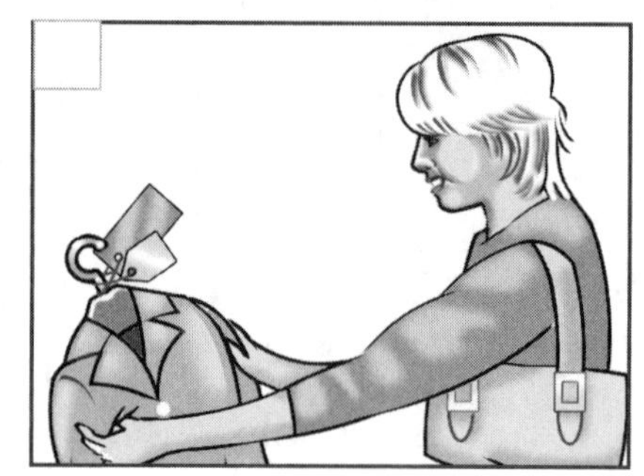

6 **Listen and read.** Cross out the six extra words. **TR: 39**

Many of the ~~lovely~~ things we buy are tested for safety.
That's good! Products should be very safe.
They should be totally safe for you and me.

When you're a good customer,
the new products you buy shouldn't break.
A famous manufacturer
should try not to make bad mistakes.

7 **Write.** Write a verse such as this one. Describe a toy or something you wear.

Is this clock waterproof?
It goes tick tock.
Let's dip the clock.
It's just a test
to make sure everything is safe.

GRAMMAR

Ming: "**Wear** a safety helmet!"	Ming: "Wear **your** safety helmet!"
Ming told me **to wear** a safety helmet.	Ming told me to wear **my** safety helmet.
Mei: "**Don't drop** the camera."	Mei: "Don't drop **my** camera!"
Mei told me **not to drop** the camera.	Mei told me not to drop **her** camera.

8 **Look and write.** Make sentences.

1
Be careful, and don't tear your pants.
2
Don't forget your homework, and enjoy your weekend!
3
Wear your safety helmet, and don't crash your bike again!

4
Don't drop my camera. Hold it with both hands!

5
Buy something useful. Don't waste money!

6
Please don't make calls. Turn off your cell phone!

1. The man told the boy to be careful. He told him not to tear his pants.
2. ______________________
3. ______________________
4. ______________________
5. ______________________
6. ______________________

9 Label the picture.

an app a key reception a text message Wi-Fi

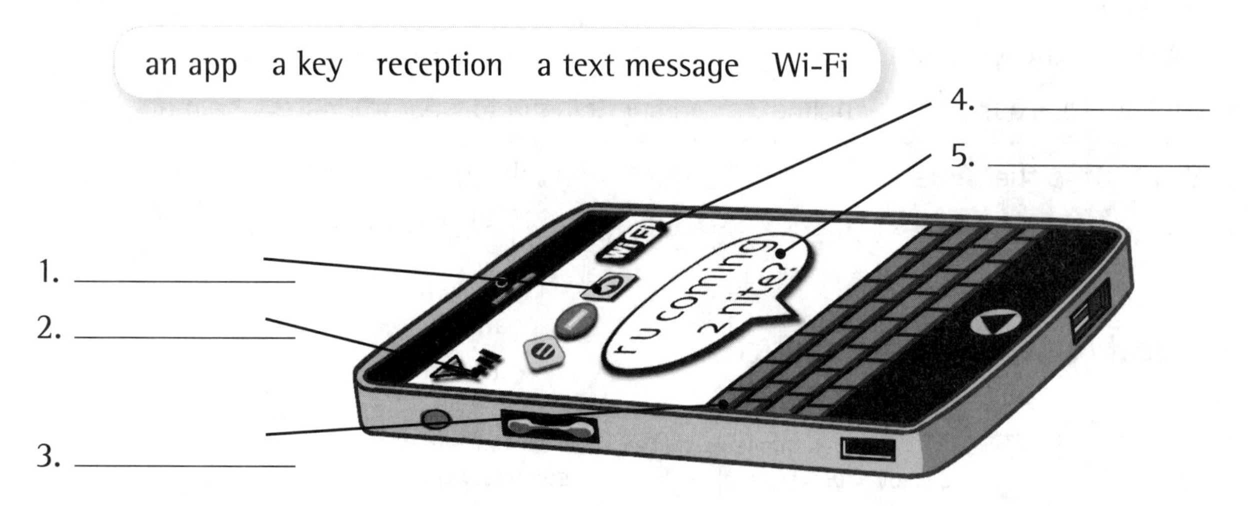

10 Match the questions and answers.

1. That's strange. I can't make any calls. What's happening? _____
2. I like to buy products that are strong and last a long time. What about you? _____
3. Excuse me. Is there Wi-Fi in this building? _____
4. Jan isn't here yet, and I don't know where she is. Should we call her? _____
5. That's a cool phone. What apps do you have? _____
6. My phone has @ on it. What does that mean? _____

a. Ah, that key is very important. You use it for e-mail addresses.
b. Maybe the reception isn't very good here. Try another room.
c. Why don't you send a text message instead? It costs less money.
d. Yes, I like things that survive wear and tear, too.
e. Yes, but you have to pay if you want to use it.
f. It has hundreds of games. I haven't tried most of them yet!

11 **What about you?** What should a good cell phone have? Write your ideas. Explain your reasons.

A cell phone should have good reception so that you can make calls from different places.
It should also have ______________ so that ______________________________.
In addition, it should have ______________ so that ______________________________.
It must have ______________ so that ______________________________.

12 **Read and write.** Write what is most important to these customers.

cost crash tests manufacturer quality

1. I'm the kind of customer who likes products that survive lots of wear and tear. I don't want products that look good but break! I want products that are good __________!
2. Injuries or accidents are terrible. Whenever I buy a car, I always check that the manufacturer tests them carefully. __________ are the most important thing for me.
3. I buy products made by a well-known company. They cost more money, but at least you know they were tested and they work. For me, a good __________ is important.
4. I'm happy with a cheap phone that makes calls and sends text messages. I don't need an expensive phone with Wi-Fi or apps. For me, __________ is very important!

13 **Read the dialogues.** Underline the correct word. Then listen to the dialogues to check your answers. **TR: 40**

A

Fatima: Dad, I **dropped** / **tore** my camera while I was taking a photo. It broke on impact.

Dad: Are you sure it's **fixed** / **broken**, Fatima? Have you **tested** / **cost** it?

Fatima: Yes, I have. It's not working.

Dad: Fatima, we bought that camera last week and it **cost** / **dropped** a lot of money!

Fatima: I know. I'm sorry, Dad. I didn't mean to **dip** / **break** it.

B

Mom: What happened to your jeans, Omar? You've **torn** / **broken** them again!

Omar: I know. I feel bad, Mom. I **dipped** / **tore** them while I was climbing a tree.

Mom: Omar, you must look after your clothes. They **cost** / **break** a lot of money!

Omar: I know. I'm really sorry, Mom. Please can you **dip** / **fix** them?

Mom: OK, I'll try. If you **test** / **tear** them again, I'll be very angry.

14 **What about you?** How good are you at taking care of your things? How can you look after them better? Write your answers in your notebook.

GRAMMAR

Questions

Katya: "Where is it?"	Katya asked	**where**	it **was**.
Katya: "What do I need?"	Katya asked	**what**	she **needed**.
Katya: "How does it work?"	Katya asked	**how**	it **worked**.

Yes / No questions

Ivan: "Do you like the apps?"	Ivan asked	**if**	we **liked** the apps.
Ivan: "Are you busy?"	Ivan asked	**if**	I **was** busy.
Ivan: "Can you fix it, Dad?"	Ivan asked	**if**	his dad **could** fix it.

15 Read and underline the correct words.

Ken and Misao were in the toy store. What did they ask the sales clerk?

1. Ken asked the clerk if she **sold** / **sells** toys for young kids.
2. Misao asked her if the toys **are** / **were** tested for safety.
3. Ken asked her what kind of teddy bears **she had** / **had she**.
4. Misao asked her if the toys **needed** / **did they need** batteries.
5. Ken asked her if **could he** / **he could** look at a teddy bear.
6. Misao asked her how much **the toys cost** / **did the toys cost**.

16 **Read and write.** Put the words in the correct order.

1. "Where is the shoe store?" where / We / the / asked / was / store / shoe
   We asked where the shoe store was.
2. "Why are the keys broken?" Dad / why / keys / the / broken / asked / were
   ____
3. "How much does it cost?" much / how / asked / cost / Katya / it
   ____
4. "Does the phone have Wi-Fi?" Dad / if / had / phone / the / Wi-Fi / asked
   ____
5. "Is it tested for safety?" was / Mom / if / asked / it / tested / safety / for
   ____
6. "Can you help me, Ivan?" I / Ivan / could / he / asked / if / me / help
   ____

17 **Listen.** Listen to the conversation. Write **T** for *True* or **F** for *False*. **TR: 41**

1. Marco said that he didn't know what to buy his mom.  
2. Wilma said that it was wrong to make something for your mom. 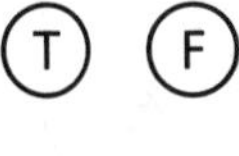
3. Marco said that his mom loved chocolate and fruit. 
4. Wilma said that she would make some food for Marco.
5. Wilma said that she would give Marco a recipe tonight. 

18 **Write.** Write the questions that Wilma and Marco asked.

1. Marco asked Wilma what he could buy.
   What can I buy?
2. He asked her what she meant.
   ____
3. He asked Wilma if her mom liked that kind of gift.
   ____
4. He asked Wilma what he could make for his mom.
   ____
5. She asked him if his mom liked chocolate and fruit.
   ____
6. He asked her if he needed many ingredients.
   ____

19 **Work with a partner.** Student 1, go to page 126. Student 2, go to page 128.

20 Listen and read. TR: 42

Don't Panic!

Splaaassshhh. Your phone drops in the bath, washtub, or pool. Now what should you do? Cell phones are extremely durable. They can survive rain, but they are not waterproof yet. Therefore, if you want to save it, you need to be quick and follow these steps!

1. Take your phone out of the water quickly. Don't turn on the phone.
2. Take out the battery and remove the SIM card, if your phone has one. This step is extremely important. Electricity does not mix with water!
3. Dry your phone carefully for ten minutes. (Note: If the phone was dropped in saltwater, clean it first with fresh water.)
4. Use a vacuum cleaner (not a hair dryer or microwave). Hold it near the phone—but not too close. Dry each part of the phone for twenty minutes. Don't switch your phone on yet.
5. Put the phone in a bowl of dry rice. Leave it overnight. Moisture will soak into the uncooked rice during the night.
6. Wait 24 hours. Then test your cell phone: insert the battery and switch it on. If nothing happens, find some dry rice and put the phone in again.

After a phone goes for a swim, most people buy a new one, but not everyone does. It is possible to save a wet phone. Just be patient and don't panic!

21 Read and write. Write **T** for *True* or **F** for *False*.

1. Cell phones can survive small drops of water.  T F
2. If you are patient, you can save a wet phone. T F
3. Fresh water is better for cell phones than saltwater. T F
4. Cook the rice before your put your phone in it. T F
5. Some people are able to save a wet phone. T F

22 **Read the text again.** Number the pictures in order (1-6).

a. ____

b. ____

c. 1

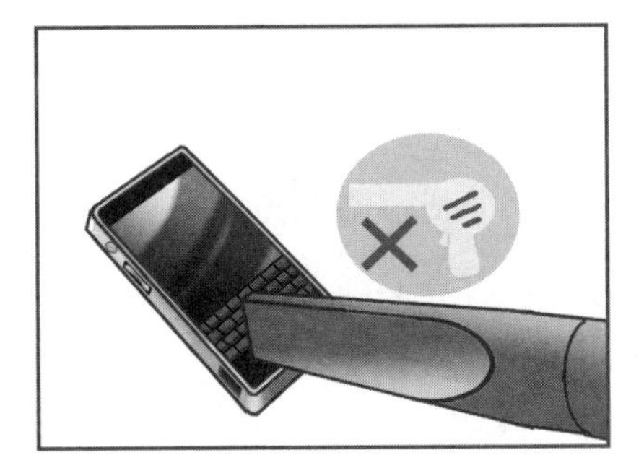

d. ____

e. ____

f. ____

23 **Read the text again.** Write how long each step takes. Circle the total.

1. Take your phone out of the water	1 minute (maximum)
2. Remove the battery and SIM card.	5 minutes
3. Dry the phone with a cloth.	________
4. Dry each part of the phone with a vacuum cleaner.	________ for each part.
5. Leave the phone in a bowl of dry rice.	________
6. Wait before you test the phone.	________

TOTAL TIME: 1 day / 2 days / 3 days

24 **Work with a partner.** Prepare and practice a role play.

Student A - You have dropped your cell phone in the water. You're in a panic!

Student B - Give your friend some advice (without looking at the text in Activity 20!)

25 **Read *Carry Your Books in Style* on page 100 of your Student Book.** How did the writer plan the writing? Read the steps.

1. First, the writer chose a product with good and bad points.
2. Next, the writer wrote down ideas about the backpack—good points and bad points. She used a chart. Read the text and complete the chart.

Product	Good Points	Bad Points
Backpack	- can carry lots of books - strong material (waterproof / survives wear and tear) - ____________ - ____________	- less cool than a leather backpack - ____________

3. After making notes about a backpack, the writer organized her notes and planned her paragraphs.

   Paragraph 1: Introduction

   Who is it for? What is it made of?

   Paragraph 2: Special features

   Why do the reviewers like the backpack? How does it compare to other backpacks?

   Paragraph 3: Conclusion

   What do the reviewers like best of all? How many stars do they give it?

4. Then, she thought of words and expressions that show emphasis: *above all, particularly, of course, in fact, really, the truth is, in addition.*

   Find these sentences. Complete them with an expression of emphasis. Check your punctuation carefully!

   a. ____________ we tested it and it doesn't tear easily.

   b. ____________ the material is waterproof.

   c. We ____________ like this backpack because it doesn't weigh a lot.

   d. ____________ leather backpacks may look cooler, but they are heavier.

   e. Carrying a heavy backpack is bad for your back, so ____________ we prefer this one.

5. Finally, she wrote the first version, called a draft, of her paragraph.

26 Before you write your own product review, read a review of a cell phone in your Student Book on page 96.

27 Choose a product that you would like to review: ______________________
Follow steps 2–5 on page 76. Write your product review in your notebook.

Introduction	Special features	Conclusions

28 **Express yourself.** Choose one of the objects below, and write a review. Plan your writing, and follow the steps on page 76. Write your new product review in your notebook.

a box of chocolates
an ice cream parlor
a pair of sneakers
a skateboard
a cell phone case
a video game

Review

1 **Play a game.** Complete the sentences and cross out the words on the cell phone.

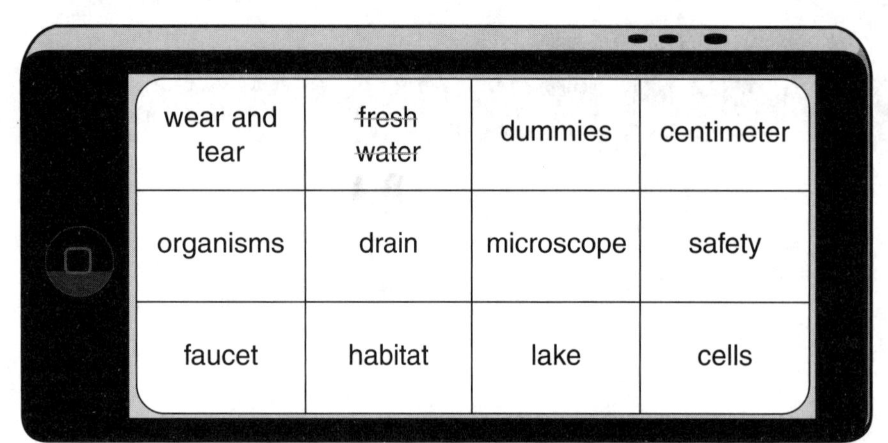

wear and tear	~~fresh water~~	dummies	centimeter
organisms	drain	microscope	safety
faucet	habitat	lake	cells

1. Salt water has salt in it. Water without salt is called fresh water.
2. Helmets, knee pads, and elbow pads are important for your ____________.
3. The place where a creature lives is called a ____________.
4. ____________ are living things. They can be plants or animals.
5. A ____________ is a body of water. It is smaller than the sea.
6. Ten millimeters is the same as one ____________.
7. ____________ is what happens when you use a product for a long time.
8. We use a __________ to see tiny creatures. It is usually made of metal and glass.
9. ____________ are statues that look like people. They are used in crash tests.
10. In your home, running water goes down the ____________.

2 **Write.** Write a sentence with each of the words you didn't cross out in Activity 1.

1. ____
2. ____

3 **Look and write.** Label the pictures.

carve ~~cost~~ crawl filter float grab leak soak

1. 
cost

2. 
____

3. 
____

4. 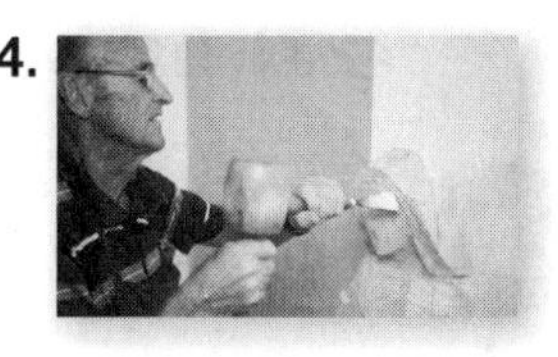
____

5. 
____

6. 
____

7. 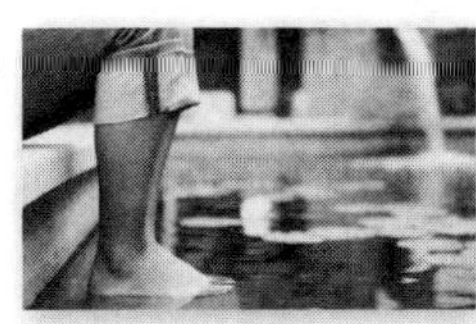
____

8. 
____

4 **Read and write.** Write what these people told you (not) to do.

1. Mom: "Sit down. Soak your feet in warm water."

   Mom told me to sit down. She told me to soak my feet in warm water.

2. Teacher: "Put on your new life jacket. Float in the pool."

   ____

3. Sister: "Crawl under the table and hide!"

   ____

4. Grandma: "Don't leave your computer on. Save electricity."

   ____

5 **Write.** Complete the sentences.

whatever whenever wherever

1. __________ I use water, I try not to waste it.
2. Mom does __________ she can to help other people.
3. Nowadays there is good Wi-Fi reception __________ you go.

6 **Match.** Connect each word with its opposite meaning.

1. normal	a. female	5. fat	e. horrible
2. male	b. tiny	6. dry	f. thin
3. enormous	c. baby	7. nice	g. rare
4. adult	d. strange	8. common	h. wet

7 **Read and write.** Write the words in the correct order.

1. A seahorse can grab grass with its long pointed pink tail. (pointed / pink / long)
2. The Lion's Mane jellyfish has ______________ tentacles. (red / huge / spotted)
3. This ________________ frog becomes gray when it's scared. (adult / amazing / green)
4. _____________ rabbits are very common animals. (white / furry / cute)

8 **Read and write.** Write what these two people asked.

Sales Assistant

1. Can I help you?
3. When did you buy it?
5. Why is the product wet?
7. Did you drop it in the lake?

Boy

2. Can you fix my camera?
4. How much will it cost to fix?
6. What is the problem?
8. Do you sell waterproof cameras?

1. She asked the customer if she could help him.
2. ____
3. ____
4. ____
5. ____
6. ____
7. ____
8. ____

9 **Read and write.** Complete the conversation.

Dad: What has Oscar been doing (do) all morning? He's been in his room for hours.

Mom: I think ______________ (he / sleep). He was very tired last night.

Oscar: Good morning! How are you?

Mom: Good morning, Oscar. It's very late. Have you been asleep?

Oscar: No, Mom. ______________ (I / do) my homework.

Dad: In bed? I hope ______________ (you / not / write) in bed!

Oscar: No, Dad. ______________ (I / read) about jellyfish. They're amazing. Did you know that ______________ (they / live) in the ocean for more than 650 million years?

10 **Read.** Check **T** for *True* and **F** for *False*.

The Ganges river dolphin is one of only four types of freshwater dolphins in the world. This beautiful gray Asian dolphin is usually found in the Ganges River. The Ganges, which begins in the frozen glaciers of the Himalayas, flows 2,510 km (1,560 miles) to the sea in Bangladesh. The river dolphin lives in the lower part of the river, where it eats shrimp and fish.

Today, it is rare to see a Ganges river dolphin. It is an endangered species for many reasons. First, the river has traveled through about forty cities, so the water has become dirty and polluted. Dams have also separated the males from the females. Boats sometimes kill the dolphins by accident. Worse, they are hunted by humans for meat. Dolphins must be protected. "Ganges" means *life*!

1. The Ganges river dolphin lives in salt water. T F ✓
2. The river dolphin lives in the lower part of the river. T F
3. Ganges river dolphins are becoming more common. T F
4. Their habitat has changed. T F
5. Some male dolphins can't find females. T F
6. Boats protect dolphins and provide safety. T F

11 **Write in your notebook.** Why is it important to protect all creatures on Earth?

Unit 7

Wonders of the Natural World

1 **Do the puzzle.** Circle the words. Then label the pictures.

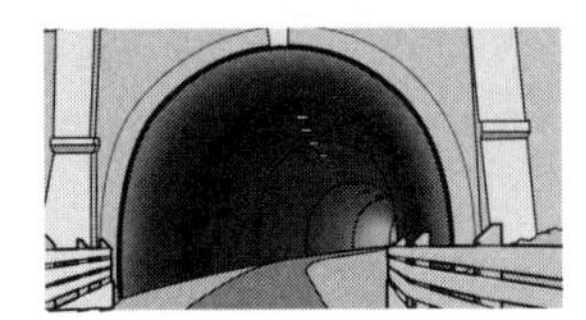 ________  ________  ________ 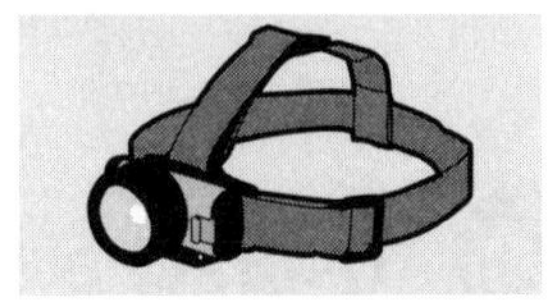 ________

A	C	C	I	D	E	N	T	E	R
S	U	H	T	R	I	P	R	D	O
C	R	A	A	C	I	S	E	K	P
R	I	S	K	S	N	L	T	M	E
L	O	C	A	T	E	R	A	T	T
E	S	E	W	R	A	L	W	C	P
N	I	N	O	E	D	G	R	E	S
N	T	D	G	A	T	O	E	D	S
U	Y	A	E	M	S	H	D	A	O
T	A	H	I	S	H	I	N	E	R
D	E	S	C	E	N	D	U	H	C

~~ACCIDENT~~	LOCATE
ASCEND	RISK
CHASE	ROPE
CROSS	SHINE
CURIOSITY	STREAMS
DESCEND	TRIP
GEAR	TUNNEL
HEADLAMP	UNDERWATER

2 **Read and match.** Match each word to its meaning.

1. ascend
2. descend
3. locate
4. trip over
5. cross
6. chase

a. go down (a mountain or hill)
b. fall over something on the ground
c. go up (a mountain or hill)
d. run after
e. find where something is
f. go to the other side of something (such as a road or bridge)

3 **Listen to the story.** Choose the correct answer. **TR: 43**

1. At first, everything was fine. What was the weather like?
   a. It was raining. b. The sun was shining.
2. What did the thieves cross?
   a. a stream b. a long tunnel
3. What safety gear did they use to ascend the mountain?
   a. a rope b. headlamps
4. What happened by accident?
   a. The gorilla dropped something. b. A thief tripped over a rock.
5. How did the gorilla look at the men when he first saw them?
   a. with curiosity b. angrily

4 **Listen.** Check the correct pronunciation of the *-ed* ending in each word. Then listen and repeat. **TR: 44**

	/t/ or /d/	/id/
1. crossed	✓	
2. ascended		✓
3. tripped (over)		
4. chased		
5. descended		
6. decided		

5 **Write in your notebook.** Add more details to the story. Use your imagination.

1. What else chased the men? When? Why?
2. Why did the gorilla look at the men with curiosity?
3. Where was the gold really located?

6 **Write and listen.** Label the pictures. Then listen and check the pictures that are mentioned in the song. **TR: 45**

a cave   a jungle   a mountain   a river   underwater   ~~a volcano~~

☐ a volcano

☐ ____________

☐ ____________

☐ ____________

☐ ____________

☐ ____________

7 **Read and listen.** Find six mistakes. Cross out the wrong word, and write the new word on the line. **TR: 46**

Let's go ~~camping~~! exploring

Let's explore! Let's go inside a cave. ____________

Let's explore! Be sure to be safe. ____________

Let's explore! There's so much to feel. ____________

Don't forget your safety hat and curiosity! ____________

We're inside a cave. ____________

We're ready to go down. ____________

What should we use to keep us safe? ____________

A hand can be used to help us descend. ____________

A headlamp can be carried to help us light our way. ____________

GRAMMAR

This tunnel The stream Safety gear Headlamps	**must / must not** **can / can't** **has to** **have to**	**be**	**entered**. **crossed** here. **checked** carefully. **turned** on.	
Why When What	**can / can't** **must / must not** **has to / have to**	the cave the chores –	**be**	**visited**? **done**? **checked**?

8 Read and match.

1. Diana Northup can often be
2. This cave is dangerous. It can't be
3. A headlamp has to be
4. Some creatures mustn't be

a. worn so that she can see in the cave.
b. found in caves. She loves to explore.
c. touched. They could hurt her hand.
d. entered without safety gear.

Diana Northup

9 Read and write. Complete the sentences.

1. Diana Northup has curiosity. She wants to know about life in this cave. That means the cave ________________ (must / visit). Caves are dangerous places, and some risks ________________ (have to / take). Northup is always careful.
2. She knows the dangers. For example, Northrup knows that the air in this cave is poisonous, so she uses a gas mask. The cave ________________ (mustn't / enter) without a gas mask.
3. Northup knows that the level of gas goes up and down. When it goes up, it is extremely dangerous. That's why a gas meter ________________ (have to / use). With this, the gas level ________________ (can / check) while she is down there.

10 **Look, match, and listen.** Match the words and phrases from Column A with those in Column B. Then listen to check your answers. **TR: 47**

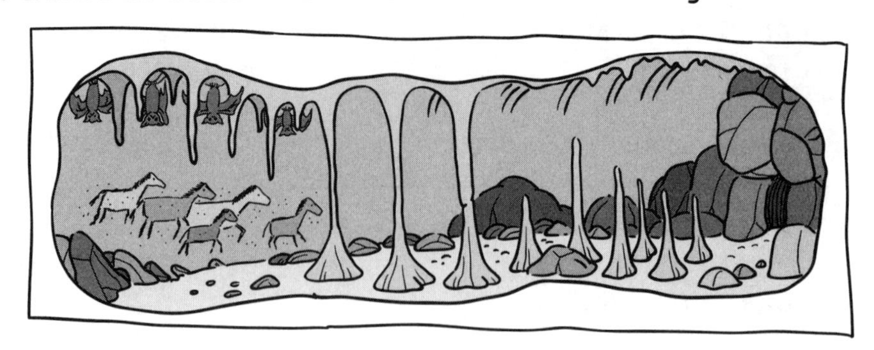

A	B
Objects in the cave	**Where they are located**
1. a painting by ancestors	a. on the right
2. bats	b. hanging from the ceiling
3. stalactites	c. at the back, on the wall
4. stalagmites	d. in the center of the cave
5. columns	e. above the painting

11 **Listen again.** Complete the sentences. **TR: 48**

1. Our ___ancestors___ often painted on cave walls.
2. A famous cave located in France has 600 ________ of animals.
3. ________ find their way without eyes and can live for 100 years.
4. ________ take thousands of years to grow.
5. ________ grow up from the ground.

12 **Match the questions and answers.** Then practice with a partner.

1. Eek! Something just flew down from the ceiling. What was it? ___
2. My great-grandfather's name was MacDonald. He was from Scotland. ___
3. Who designed the columns on that building? They're beautiful. ___
4. Why don't we make a painting for Dad's birthday? ___

a. Really? One of my ancestors is from there, too.
b. It's a good idea, but I'm really bad at art.
c. That? Oh, it was just a bat. There are probably hundreds up there.
d. They were made by a famous Greek architect. They're incredibly cool.

13 **Read.** Underline the correct word.

Son Doong Cave is ***located* / *ascended*** in Vietnam. It contains 150 small caves, waterfalls, and a jungle. Parts of the cave are so big that a jumbo jet could fly through it! Explorers take many ***risks* / *safety gear*** in this cave. Anything could happen by accident: they could trip over rocks in the dark, get lost in a ***tunnel* / *rope***, or be ***chased* / *risked*** by an animal in the jungle. Fortunately, ever since explorers ***descended* / *chased*** into the cave, they have skillfully used ropes to ***trip over* / *cross*** rivers, hiked for days, and swum ***underwater* / *underground***. Now they are tired, so they stop for a rest. They ***shine* / *chase*** their headlamps on the cave walls and look around. It is awesome. Huge stalagmites and stalactites can be seen. Up above them, bats are flying around. After taking photos, they check their ***safety gear* / *curiosity*** and continue their journey.

14 **Read and write.** Read the text in Activity 13. Answer the questions.

1. Name two safety gear objects you can find in the text.

____

2. Name two things that could happen by accident to explorers inside the cave.

____

3. Name two things that explorers find in the cave.

____

15 **What can you say?** Circle all the correct letters.

1. Cross ___.	(a.) the road	(b.) a stream	c. a door	(d.) a bridge
2. ___ chased the man.	a. A ball	b. The police	c. A dog	d. A thief
3. ___ a painting.	a. Make	b. Buy	c. Look at	d. Watch
4. ___ shone.	a. A candle	b. A flashlight	c. Curiosity	d. The sun

16 **What about you?** Write true sentences. Use words and phrases from Activity 15.

1. ____
2. ____
3. ____
4. ____

GRAMMAR

Heights		**me**	scared.
Motocross	**make**	**you**	excited.
It	**makes**	**him / her**	proud.
The party	**made**	**us**	happy.
Playing tennis		**them**	tired.

17 **Read and write.** Write a follow-up sentence using the words in parentheses.

1. Marcelo broke his leg by accident, and he couldn't play soccer. (It / sad)
   It made him sad.
2. When we ascended the mountain, I felt sick at the top. (The height / dizzy)
   ______
3. My friend Sara gets worried when we play near the tunnel. (Playing / nervous)
   ______
4. We bought Uncle Mario a new headlamp for his birthday. (The headlamp / happy)
   ______
5. I won a prize in school. Mom and Dad were so proud of me. (I / proud)
   ______
6. Hmm! I feel hungry when I look at that candy bar! (Looking / hungry)
   ______

18 **Write.** Describe what makes—or made—you feel this way.

1. Angry: ______
2. Bored: ______
3. Happy: ______
4. Excited: ______

19 **Listen to the conversation.** Check **T** for *True* or **F** for *False*. **TR: 49**

1. Trash cans are on the site. ☑T ○F
2. Trash must be put in the correct bins. ○T ○F
3. Maps have to be bought. ○T ○F
4. Animals must not be fed. ○T ○F

20 **Look and write.** Remember the story in Activity 19? What do the signs mean?

8 p.m - 6 a.m.

B

Do not chase

at night	biodegradable bin	can	can't	chase
have to	must	must not	put	take

1. Trash must not be put in the bins at night.
2. Biodegradable trash ______________________.
3. Photos ______________________.
4. Animals ______________________.

21 **Write.** Write the rule and explain the reason.

1. fires / light → campsite unsafe
   Fires can't be lit because they make the campsite unsafe.
2. music / play / at night → visitors angry
   ____
3. bikes / ride / slowly → animals nervous
   ____
4. helmets / wear → cyclists safe
   ____

22 **Think and write in your notebook.** Imagine you are the owner of a campsite. What rules would you make? Why?

23 Listen and read. TR: 50

Finding a Lost World

Scientists need curiosity for their job. Mireya Mayor has plenty! She has traveled to Namibia to study leopards, been chased by gorillas in central Africa, swum with sharks, and been underwater with a huge squid. She has also discovered new species, including a mouse lemur she found in Madagascar by accident.

Scientists also need strength. Mayor is incredibly strong. Once she ascended a huge table mountain (*tepui*) deep in the jungle of South America. Let's join her on the trip to Mount Roraima, a *tepui* located on the border of Guyana, Brazil, and Venezuela.

For three weeks, Mayor and a team of scientists and climbers traveled on foot through the jungle. It was hard work. Tired, hot, and bitten by bugs, they finally arrived at the foot of the *tepui*. It rose 2.7 kilometers (9,000 feet) above them. Mayor had never climbed rocks before, and she was afraid of heights! Nevertheless, she ascended the dangerous *tepui* by rope for two days, stopping overnight to sleep in a "tent" that hung in the air above the clouds. The next day, when Mayor reached the top of the *tepui*, she knew her journey was worth every step. Once again, her curiosity had taken her to a lost world, full of strange and unknown species!

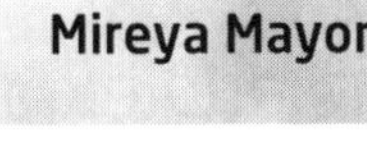

Mireya Mayor

24 Read and match.

1. Mireya Mayor is	a. and strength.
2. She has both curiosity	b. made her very happy.
3. To ascend the *tepui*, she	c. a scientist.
4. Her tent was not	d. is above the clouds.
5. The top of Mount Roraima	e. on the ground.
6. Reaching the top	f. needed safety gear.

25 **Answer the questions.** Use information from the passage in Activity 23 to answer the questions.

1. What does Mayor have that scientists need for their job?
   Curiosity
2. Where did she travel to find gorillas?
   ______
3. What is a *tepui*?
   ______
4. What creatures caused her problems on the walk through the jungle?
   ______
5. Why did the trip up the mountain make her scared?
   ______

26 **Reread.** Read the third paragraph of Activity 23. What details does the writer add to create suspense and interest in the story? Complete the chart.

Where? When? Why? How? How long? With whom?

Main Events	Supporting Details
1. Mayor hiked through the jungle.	on foot (how); for three weeks (how long); with a team (with whom)
2. She arrived at the foot of the *tepui*.	
3. She ascended the *tepui*.	
4. She slept in a tent.	

27 **Work with a partner.** Discuss Mireya Mayor's adventures. Which ones would (or wouldn't) you like to try? Why?

28 **Read *Search for a Gorilla* on page 120 of your Student Book.** How did the writer plan her writing? Read the steps.

1. First, the writer chose an adventure to write about: a difficult hike in the jungle.
2. Next, she read about the adventure. She listed what happened to the explorer and the order in which the events happened. She used a flow chart to do this.

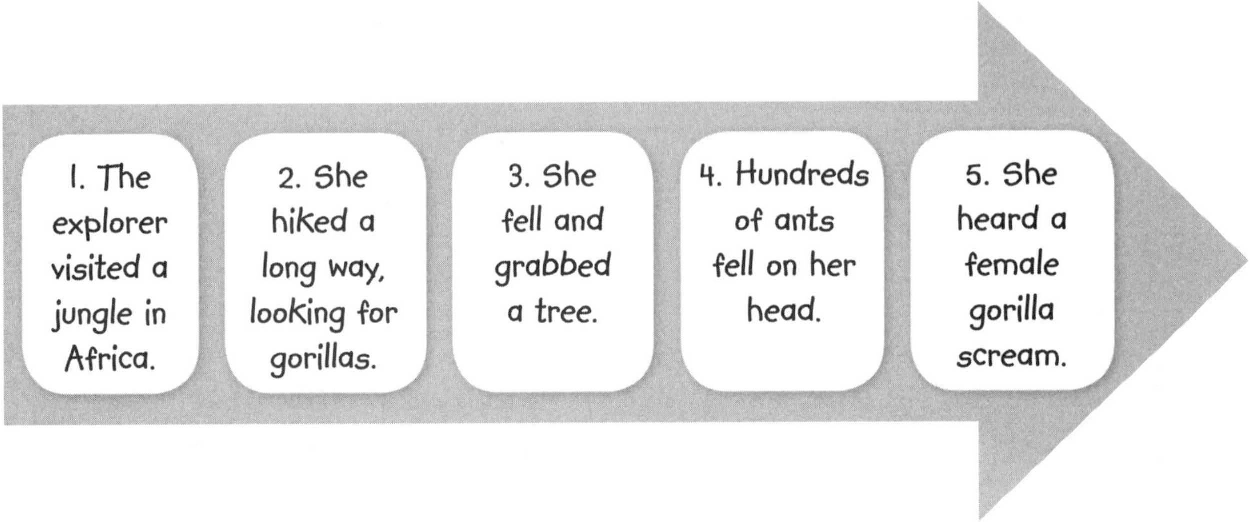

1. The explorer visited a jungle in Africa.	2. She hiked a long way, looking for gorillas.	3. She fell and grabbed a tree.	4. Hundreds of ants fell on her head.	5. She heard a female gorilla scream.

3. Next, the writer thought of words and expressions that show time:

   first/then/next *suddenly* *at one point* *immediately*

4. Then she combined information in her chart and some expressions of time. Write three examples of time that you find in her paragraphs.

   a. At one point, when she was hiking through mud, she fell.

   b. ______________________________

   c. ______________________________

5. Next, she thought of ways to create suspense in the story and make it seem real for the reader. She included details that answered the questions *when, where, why, how,* and *how long.* She also described the following:

   - the temperature
   - the trail
   - what Mayor did while she was falling
   - the number of ants
   - what the ants were doing
   - how Mayor felt

6. Finally, she wrote her first version, called a draft, of her paragraph.

29 **Choose another adventure.** Look at Activity 18 in your Student Book. What happened? Complete the flow chart.

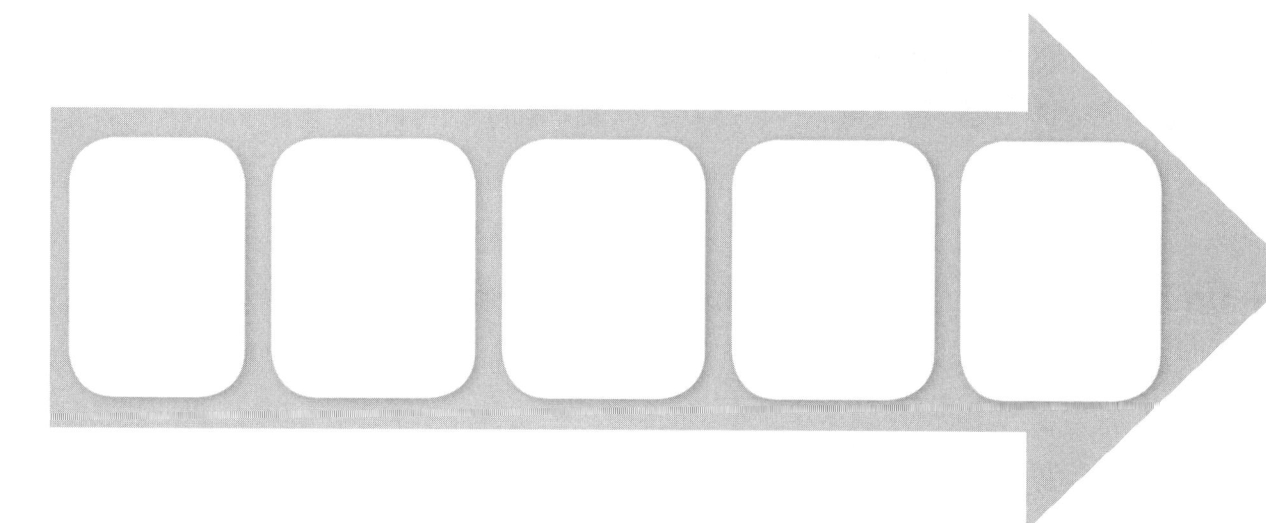

30 **Now follow steps 3-6 on page 92.** Write your paragraph in your notebook.

31 **Express yourself.** Choose one of the topics below and write a new paragraph. Plan your writing and follow the steps on page 92. Write your new paragraph in your notebook. Check that your paragraph has time expressions and that there are enough details to create suspense.

How you broke a bone
How you got dirty one time
Something that happened on a camping trip
An accident you once had
A time when you were scared
Something funny that happened

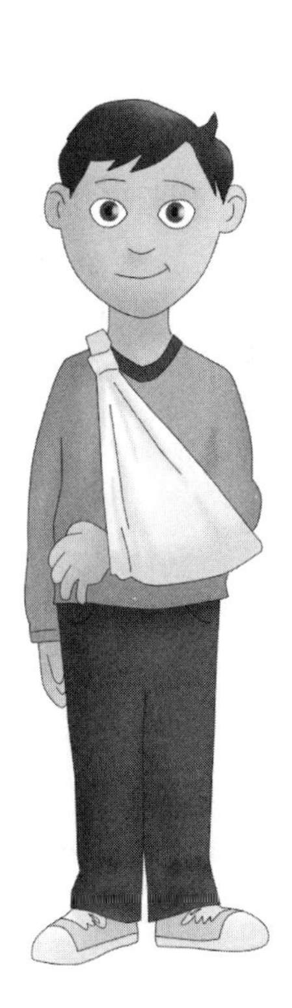

Unit 8

Robots Rule

1 **Do a puzzle.** Find the words and the secret message!

command
companion
complex
control
dangerous
feature
information
mobile
precise
program
remote control
respond to
~~robot~~
science fiction
social
task

Scrambled word	Answer
OTROB	r o b o t (16, 3)
DASGENROU	_ _ _ _ _ _ _ _ _ (7)
CODMANM	_ _ _ _ _ _ _
CALSIO	_ _ _ _ _ _ (9)
NAICOPMON	_ _ _ _ _ _ _ _ _
TEEFARU	_ _ _ _ _ _ _ (15, 8, 1)
SPREDNO OT	_ _ _ _ _ _ _ _ _ (6)
LEOCXMP	_ _ _ _ _ _ _ (2)
MINNAITORFO	_ _ _ _ _ _ _ _ _ _ _ (11)
CONRLTO	_ _ _ _ _ _ _ (13)
LEOMIB	_ _ _ _ _ _ (10)
GMROARP	_ _ _ _ _ _ _ (12)
RETMOE TONCLOR	_ _ _ _ _ _ _ _ _ _ _ _ _ (5)
RECPSEI	_ _ _ _ _ _ _ (14)
KAST	_ _ _ _
SECECIN TOCFIIN	_ _ _ _ _ _ _ _ _ _ _ _ _ _ (4)

_ _ b _ _ _ (1 2 3 4 5 6) _ _ _ _ (7 8 9 10) _ _ _ _ v _ r! (11 12 13 14 15 16)

2 **Listen and write.** Circle the correct answer. **TR: 51**

1. Why doesn't David want to go to the movie?
   He doesn't like a. comedies. b. science fiction.
2. What did the scientist program the robot to do?
   He programmed the robot to do a. tasks in the house. b. the scientist's work.
3. What happens after a while?
   The robot a. commands the scientist. b. doesn't respond to the scientist.
4. How does the robot become dangerous?
   It a. eats computer information. b. starts to eat people.
5. Why does David tell Sam to stop?
   Sam is telling a. too many details. b. details that aren't very precise.

3 **Read and write.** Complete the sentences.

complex mobile ~~precise~~ remote control

1. Robots are good at tasks in factories because they're precise.
2. Robots can go many places, including underwater, because they're __________.
3. We can control them when they are in other places by __________.
4. They are useful for tasks that are too difficult or __________ for humans.

command programmed respond to social

5. Robots can be __________ to send us information from the moon.
6. They do __________ tasks, too. For example, they're good companions for the elderly.
7. We can __________ them to do tasks in the home, such as cleaning.
8. Some robots behave like humans. They can laugh, cry, and __________ jokes!

4 **Write a short paragraph in your notebook.** Choose one job that is mentioned in Activity 3. Imagine a movie in which a robot went out of control. Write what happened!

5 **Look and write.** Match each picture to a sentence from the song. Then draw pictures to show the two extra sentences.

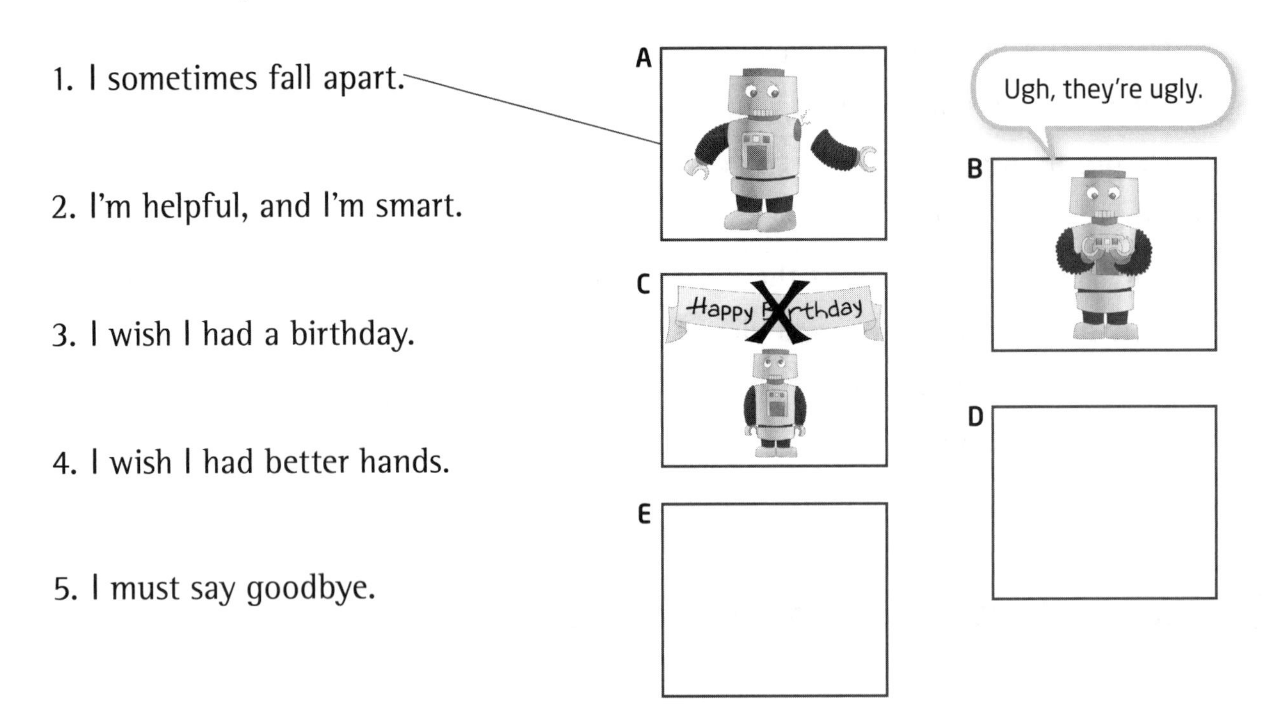

1. I sometimes fall apart.
2. I'm helpful, and I'm smart.
3. I wish I had a birthday.
4. I wish I had better hands.
5. I must say goodbye.

6 **Listen, read, and write.** Listen to the words that rhyme in each column. **TR: 52**

1	2	3	4	5
~~commands~~	told	heart	steel	goodbye
hands	gold	apart	real	cry
stands	old	smart	feel	die

Now listen to the song. Write the correct word from each column in the song. **TR: 53**

Now, I am a robot.
I follow all commands.
But I wish I had more features.
I wish I had better __________.
Now, I am a robot.
I do what I am __________.
But I wish I had a birthday.
Then again, I never will get __________.

Now, I am a robot.
made of wires and __________.
I always say the same thing
if you ask me how I __________.
Now, I am a robot,
and I must say __________.
But even when I'm sad,
I am programmed not to __________.

GRAMMAR

I		I	**had**	a big house with a yard.
You	**wish**	you	**were**	an engineer.
We		we	**could**	speak English.
They		it	**would**	stop raining!
He		he	**didn't have**	so many tasks to do.
She	**wishes**	she	**could**	have a birthday.
The robot		people	**weren't**	so complex!

7 **Listen and draw lines.** Match each person with two pictures. **TR: 54**

Keiko

Mei

Ming

A

B
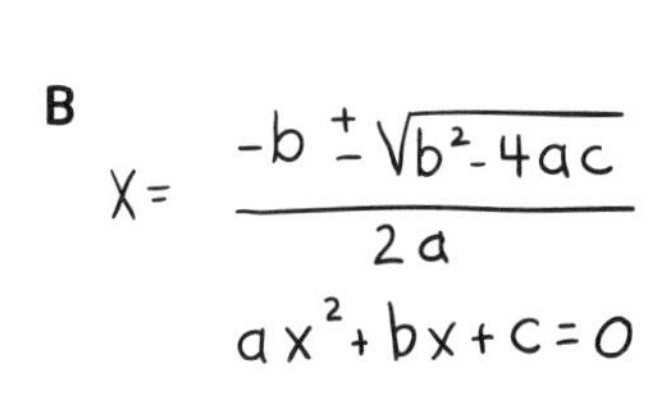

C

D
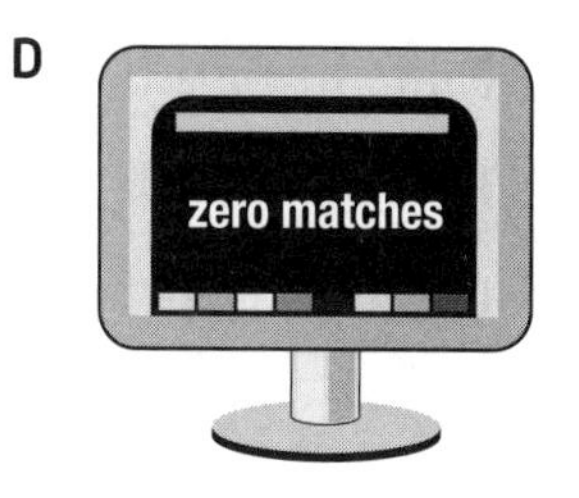

E

F

G

H

8 **Listen to the presentation.** Check **T** for *True* or **F** for *False*. **TR: 55**

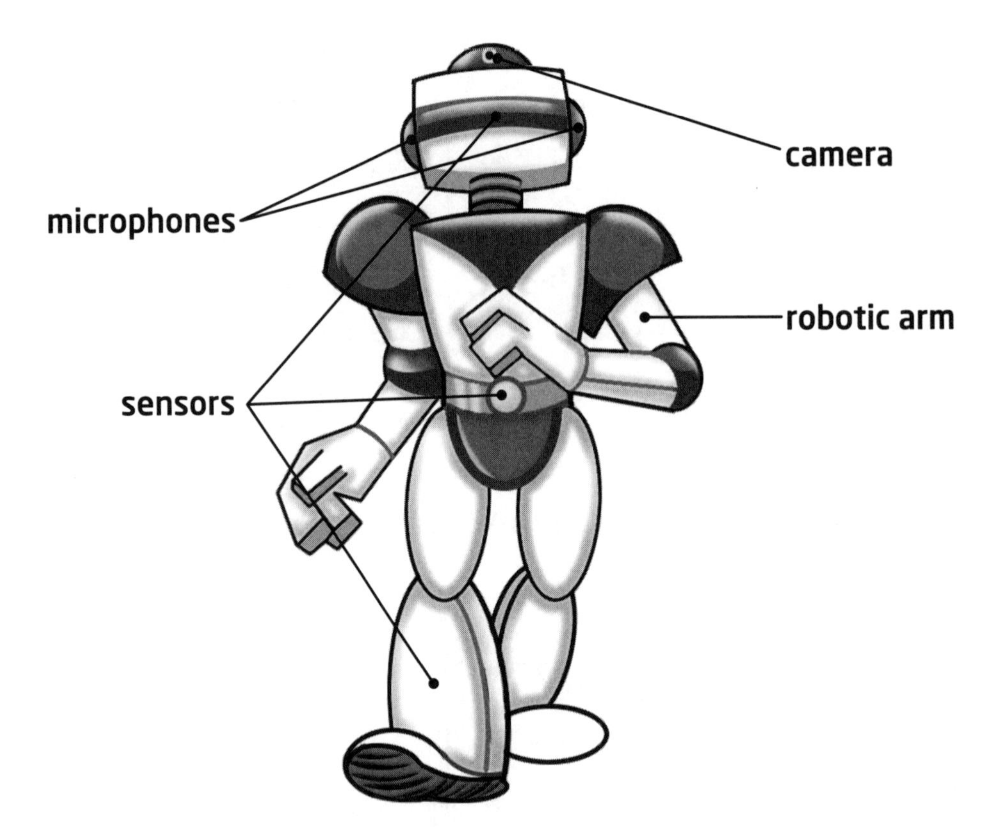

1. Marvin can dance and sing. ☑T ⓕ
2. He can speak two languages: English and Spanish. Ⓣ ⓕ
3. He works in hospitals. Ⓣ ⓕ
4. Marvin can climb stairs. Ⓣ ⓕ
5. His robotic arm is more complex than a mechanical arm. Ⓣ ⓕ

9 **Listen and write.** Listen to the presentation again. Number the order that the kids mention these features (1–4). Write where the features are located. **TR: 56**

Features	Where are the features located?
☐ facial recognition	____________________
[1] voice recognition	in the microphones
☐ laser	____________________
☐ sensor	____________________

10 **Read and write.** Match the features and their functions.

Features	Functions
1. Voice recognition	a. To help the robot lift and move objects.
2. Facial recognition	b. To help the robot understand when someone speaks.
3. Lasers	c. To help the robot feel, smell, and touch things.
4. A mechanical arm	d. To help the robot know who you are when it sees you.
5. Sensors	e. To help the robot climb stairs.

11 **Write.** Imagine your own robot. Describe it. Answer the questions.

1. What is your robot's name?
   ____
2. Who uses your robot and why?
   ____
3. What features does it have? ______________________________
4. Where are the robot's features? ______________________________
5. What do these features enable it to do? ______________________________

12 **Read and write.** Write what these things have in common.

companions   dangerous   features   places to find information   ~~precise~~   tasks

1. a calculator, a ruler, a digital watch: They are all precise.
2. my best friend, Grandpa's dog, my mom: ______________________________
3. extreme sports, hungry sharks, big waves: ______________________________
4. ears, eyes, nose, mouth: ______________________________
5. homework, chores, projects: ______________________________
6. the Internet, a book, a dictionary: ______________________________

GRAMMAR

Classroom robots	**will be**	**taught**	to help us in class.	
They	**won't be**	**programmed**	to do our homework.	
Where	**will**	the new robot		**built**?
What		he/she/it	**be**	**called**?
When		you		**told** more about it?
Why	**won't**	they		**given** voice recognition?
Will	robots	**be**	**given**	facial recognition?

13 **Read and write.** Complete the paragraph.

Great news! Our teacher is planning a party for us! The party ___will be held___ (hold) at the end of the school year. Our parents ______________ (invite). First, they ______________ (show) around the school. However, they ______________ (not / take) to the new swimming pool because it ______________ (not / finish) in time. After that, everyone in class ______________ (ask) to show them some classwork. Then we ______________ (offer) free drinks, but food ______________ (not / serve).

14 **Read and write.** Ask questions about the party described in Activity 13.

1. When / hold / party? When will the party be held?
2. Who / invite? ______________
3. Where / parents / take? ______________
4. Why / they / not show / the new pool? ______________
5. Parents / give / drinks? ______________
6. People / offer / food? ______________

15 **Read.** Circle the correct meaning.

1. I'm worried that I didn't pass the test. I wish I knew the results!
   a. I don't know the results. b. I didn't know the results.
2. Ivan has been doing his homework for hours. He wishes he weren't so slow.
   a. Ivan wasn't slow before. b. Ivan is taking a long time right now.
3. Olga wishes she could find her glasses. She has looked everywhere.
   a. She can't find them now. b. She couldn't find them earlier.

16 **Read and write.** Complete the sentences. Then match each to one of the sentences in Activity 15.

☐ a. I'm sure you haven't lost them. They will be found (They / find) soon.

☐ b. Don't worry. __________ (You / tell) tomorrow. I'm sure you passed!

☐ c. The task __________ (do) soon. Then he can go out with his friends.

17 **Work with a partner.** Make sentences about the pictures.

be taller	dance and sing	eat ice cream
have different features	mechanical arm	work in a factory

18 **Listen and read.** If you see words you don't know, try to guess. **TR: 57**

Robot Zoo

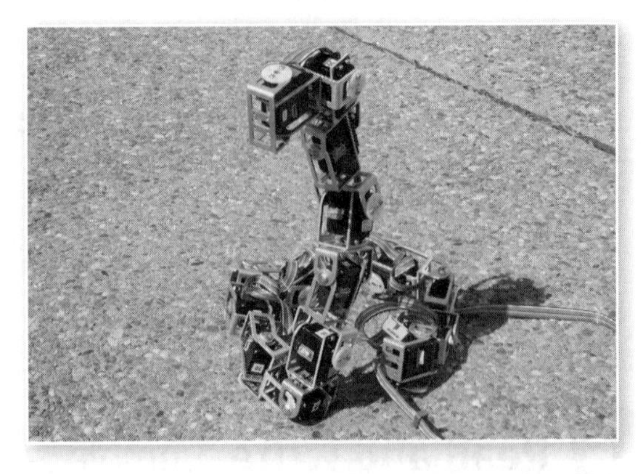

Snake-bot

Every year, scientists develop robots that will do more and more complex tasks. They are designing robots that will be extremely mobile. They want robots that can perform tasks while they are in the air, hanging from a ceiling, or in fast-moving water. Hummingbirds, bats, lobsters, and other creatures can already do these things. To design the robots, scientists copy animals!

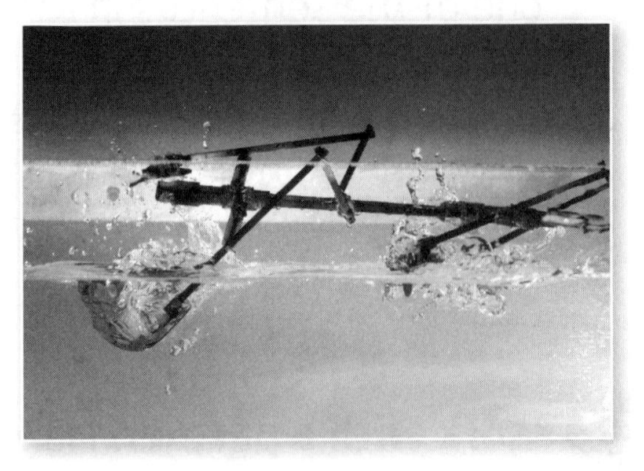

Water Runner

A popular design is the "snake-bot," which NASA has already tested. These snake robots will one day explore the surface of Mars where they could enter tiny cracks in the ground and crawl over rocks without tripping. On Earth, they could fight fires or clean drains. The Water Runner is another interesting robot that copies animal movements. It is based on the amazing basilisk lizard, a creature that runs across water to escape predators. Perhaps one day this water robot will be programmed to bring you a drink while you float in the pool!

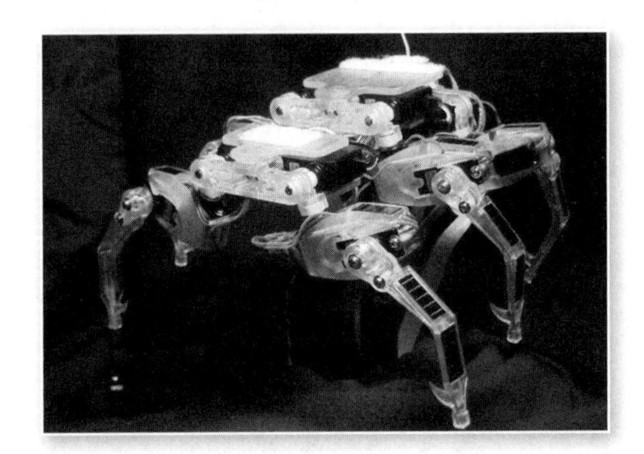

Spider-bot

Scientists are also developing "frog-bots" that jump over huge obstacles and "fly-bots" that walk upside down on the ceiling. There are also "spider-bots," "lobster-bots," and even "cockroach-bots!" Last but not least, scientists are planning a nanobot (a microscopic robot) that will eat mites and germs. Imagine—these robots could stop you from getting a cold one day!

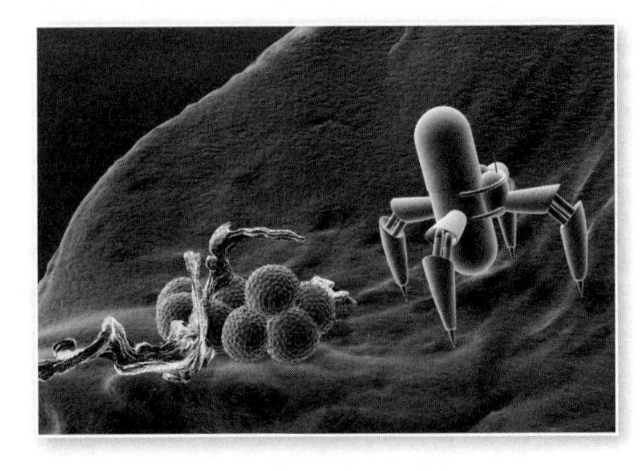

Nanobot

19 **Read and answer.** Underline the words or phrases that correctly complete each sentence.

1. Scientists are learning to make robots that *look* / *move* like animals.
2. The "snake-bot" *has* / *hasn't* been designed.
3. The Water Runner *travels underwater* / *crosses water* like a basilisk lizard.
4. We *can* / *can't* see a nanobot with the human eye.
5. Scientists might use nanobots to provide better *health* / *weather* for humans.

20 **Read.** Complete the chart. Write what each robot can do.

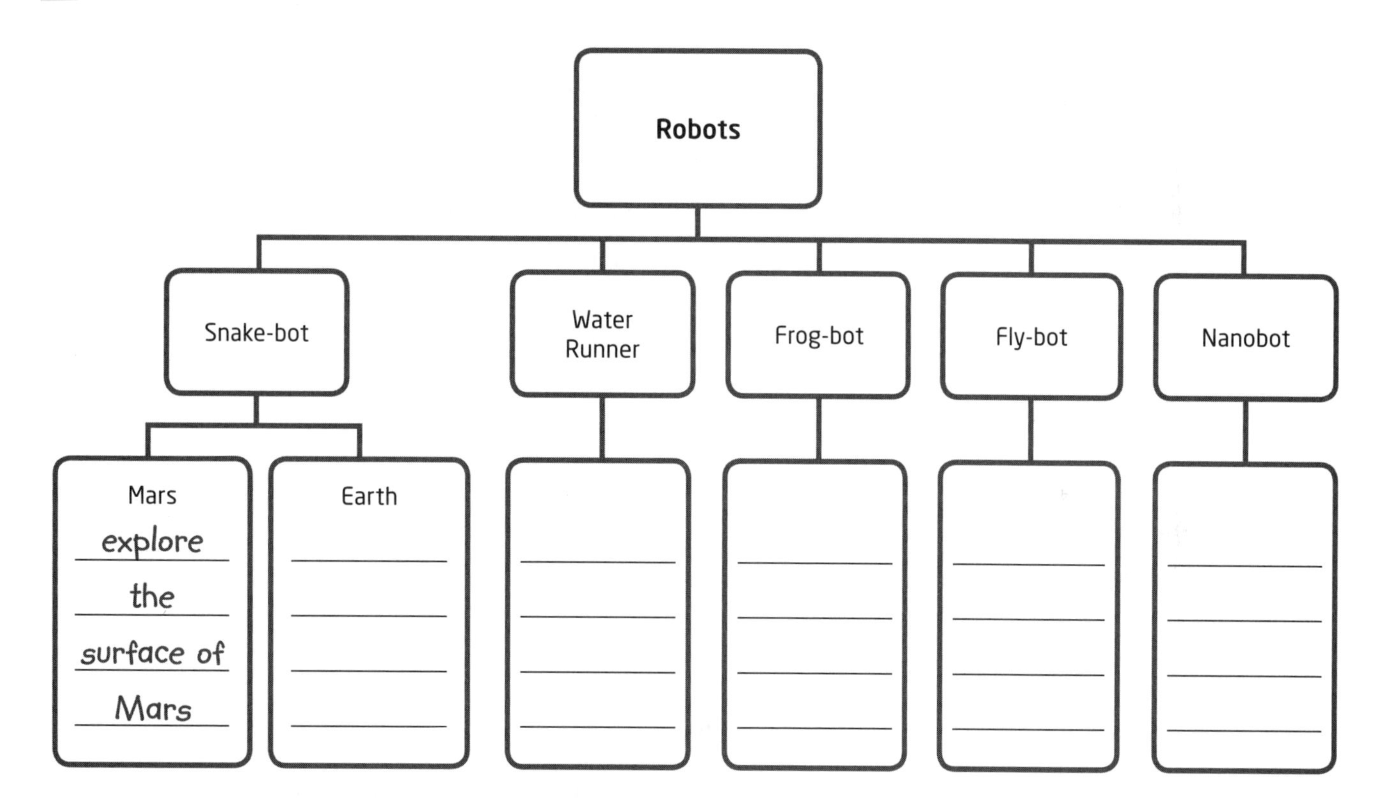

21 **Work with a partner.** Discuss ways people could use the animal robots described in Activity 18.

> How can we use lobster-bots?

> We could program lobster-bots to clean our oceans.

22 **Read *Future Bots: Ready or Not?* on page 136 of your Student Book.** How did the writer plan her writing? Read the steps.

1. First, the writer chose a topic that has at least two advantages and disadvantages. She chose the following situation: *What would happen if robots could think for themselves?*
2. Next, the writer read some information on artificial intelligence (AI). She learned what it is and what robots will be able to do with AI.
3. Then she wrote down a list of advantages and disadvantages. She asked herself the following questions: How would robots with AI be good? What bad things could happen? She used a T-chart to organize her ideas. Complete the chart.

Advantages	Disadvantages
If an explorer robot finds something interesting in space, then it can make a decision.	They might do things we don't want.
______________________	They won't know how humans behave.
______________________	______________________
______________________	______________________
	______________________

4. Then she thought of words and expressions that show advantages and disadvantages:

   on the one hand   *on the other hand*

   one (dis)advantage is   *another (dis)advantage is*

5. Complete the following sentences from the paragraph in your Student Book.
   a. These robots will be able to think for themselves and do things without us. ______________________ this is positive.
   b. ______________________ when a social robot breaks, it will know how to fix itself.
   c. ______________________ there are risks.
   d. ______________________ they might do things we don't want them to do.
6. Finally, she wrote a first version, called a draft, of her paragraph.

23 **Look at Activity 18 in your Student Book.** Plan your writing. What do you know about social robots as companions? What can they do? What tasks do they perform? What features do they have? Make notes.

24 **Write about the advantages and disadvantages of social robots as companions.** Follow steps 2–6 on page 104. Write your paragraph in your notebook.

Advantages	Disadvantages

25 **Express yourself.** Choose one of the topics below, and write a paragraph that contains at least two advantages and two disadvantages. Use words and expressions to show advantages and disadvantages. Plan your writing, and follow the steps on page 104. Write your new paragraph in your notebook.

Living in an apartment
Being the oldest or youngest child in the family
Advertisements
Watching TV

Unit 9

Amazing Adventures at Sea

1 **Do the puzzle.** Find the secret message!

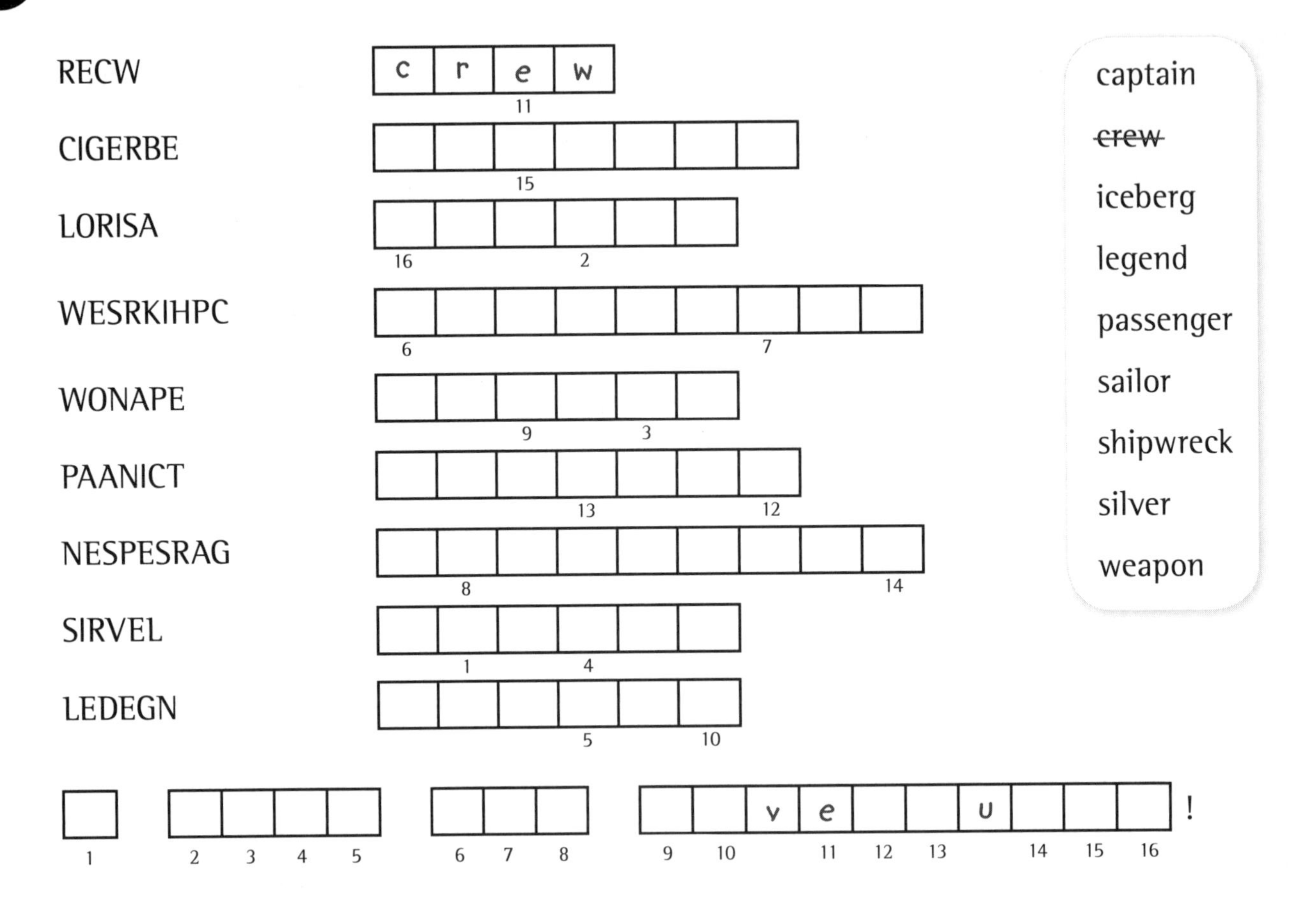

Scrambled word	Answer boxes	Numbered boxes
RECW	c r e w	11
CIGERBE	_ _ _ _ _ _ _	15
LORISA	_ _ _ _ _ _	16, 2
WESRKIHPC	_ _ _ _ _ _ _ _ _	6, 7
WONAPE	_ _ _ _ _ _	9, 3
PAANICT	_ _ _ _ _ _ _	13, 12
NESPESRAG	_ _ _ _ _ _ _ _ _	8, 14
SIRVEL	_ _ _ _ _ _	1, 4
LEDEGN	_ _ _ _ _ _	5, 10

Word box:
- captain
- ~~crew~~
- iceberg
- legend
- passenger
- sailor
- shipwreck
- silver
- weapon

Secret message:

_ (1)   _ _ _ _ (2 3 4 5)   _ _ _ (6 7 8)   _ _ v e _ _ u _ _ _ (9 10 _ 11 12 13 _ 14 15 16)!

2 **Label the pictures.**

____

____

____

____

____

3 **Read and write.** Complete the sentences. Choose the correct form.

capture / capturing / captured
dive / diving / ~~dove~~
drown / drowning / drowned
sink / sinking / sank

1. When the explorer __dove__ to the underwater cave, he wore safety gear.
2. Suddenly there was a storm. The ship ________ to the bottom of the ocean.
3. The pirates ________ many sailors and passengers, but two boys escaped.
4. Yesterday in the pool, we learned how to save someone who is ________.

4 **Listen.** Check **T** for *True* and **F** for *False*. **TR: 58**

1. Mari and the other passengers were scared. (T) ✓ (F)
2. The captain told everyone to keep calm. (T) (F)
3. A passenger dove in the water. (T) (F)
4. The boat sank. (T) (F)
5. Mari went in a lifeboat. (T) (F)

5 **Read.** Circle the option that does not belong.

1. Passengers travel
   a. on trains. (b.) on shipwrecks. c. in cars.
2. A crew works on
   a. a ship. b. a plane. c. a legend.
3. Sometimes, people are attacked by
   a. cargo. b. pirates. c. animals.
4. Many things are made of silver. For example:
   a. medals. b. earrings. c. sweaters.

6 **What about you?** Work with a partner. Discuss the questions.

1. Which types of transport have you been a passenger on/in? Name some.
2. What does the crew on an airplane do? Name some jobs they do.
3. Do you know a legend? Tell the story.

7 **Match.** Match each word to the picture it describes.

captain crew diver iceberg shipwreck treasure

a. ______________ c. ______________ e. ______________

b. ______________ d. ______________ f. ______________

8 **Listen to the song.** Number the order in which you hear each word. **TR: 59**

☐	captain	☐	dive	☐	shipwreck
☐	crew	☐	icebergs	☐	silver

9 **Listen.** Listen to the song again. Choose the correct meaning of each expression. **TR: 60**

1. Local legend says. . . .
   - a. People from this place often tell a story. It is true.
   - (b.) People from this place often tell a story. It might not be true.
2. I love sunken treasure like flowers love rain.
   - a. I really like sunken treasure.
   - b. I feel like a flower when I find treasure.
3. Here we go!
   - a. We could go over here.
   - b. We're leaving now.

GRAMMAR

As soon as	Omar finished his homework, I got on the ship,	he called me. I felt dizzy!
Omar called me I felt dizzy	**as soon as**	he finished his homework. I got on the ship!

10 **Read and write.** Join the sentences.

1. The passengers and the crew were on the ship. The ship left for a seven-day trip.

   The ship left for a seven-day trip ______ as soon as the passengers and the crew were on the ship.

2. The ship hit some rocks near the island. The electricity went off.

   As soon as ______________________.

3. The electricity went off. The passengers knew there was a problem.

   As soon as ______________________.

4. The ship began to sink. Many passengers put on their life jackets.

   ______________ as soon as ______________.

5. Some passengers dove in the water. The captain blew the whistle.

   ______________ as soon as ______________.

6. Lifeboats and helicopters reached the ship. Most passengers left safely.

   As soon as ______________________.

11 **Write.** Imagine you were on the ship described in Activity 10. Complete the following sentences.

1. As soon as my family and I got on the ship, we ______________.
2. I began to feel scared as ______________.
3. As soon as the electricity went off, I ______________.
4. I sent a text message as ______________.
5. As soon as I got home, I ______________.

12 Match the questions and answers.

1. How was your test, Gerardo? Did you do well? d
2. Please can we go swimming in the sea, Dad? ____
3. Is it true that Blackbeard used to decorate his ships with bones? ____
4. These are beautiful flowers. Can we take them home on the plane, Mom? ____
5. Why can't you do your math homework? What's the problem? ____
6. Those boys are diving near the rocks. Is that safe? ____

a. It's really difficult. Some questions are impossible!
b. Whoever told you that is incorrect. It's just a legend about a pirate!
c. No, it isn't. They could drown or have a serious accident.
d. Yes, I did. I got all the answers correct!
e. No, it's unsafe out there. A big storm is coming.
f. I don't think so. It's illegal to take plants and seeds to other countries.

13 **Read and write.** Write an expression that means the same thing as each underlined word or phrase.

correct   impossible   ~~it is possible~~   safe   that's incorrect   unsafe

1. a. I read that kids can hear some sounds that adults can't hear. Is that possible?
   b. Yes, <u>they can</u>. Kids can do lots of things that adults can't do.
   it is possible
2. a. Did you know that a Japanese city sank 3,000 years ago? People dive there.
   b. Actually, <u>that's wrong</u>. It sank 2,000 years ago, but it's still amazing!
   ____
3. a. Is it true that bees only attack people when they feel scared?
   b. Yes. People say they're <u>dangerous</u>, but you're <u>fine</u> if you leave them alone.
   dangerous: ____________ fine: ____________
4. a. My teacher said that some icebergs are green or blue. Is that true?
   b. Yes, it is. At first, I thought it was <u>not possible</u>, but she's <u>right</u>. I've seen them.
   not possible: ____________ right: ____________

14 **Read.** Underline the correct words.

Moonfleet is one of my favorite books. The story begins in a small town by the sea called Moonfleet. A popular ***weapon / legend*** says the famous ***pirate / crew*** Blackbeard is buried under Moonfleet church and his ghost walks around at night! A boy named John discovers a cave and learns that people hide ***illegal / impossible*** cargo under the church. They walk around at night, not Blackbeard! Blackbeard really existed—in 1718 he was ***captured / captain*** of four stolen ships and 300 ***silver / sailors***—but now John knows that the town legend is ***correct / incorrect.***

15 **Listen to the rest of the story.** Answer the questions. **TR: 61**

1. When does the storm happen? The storm happens as soon as the ship leaves the coast.
2. What do people think will happen to the ship? __________
3. How do some passengers escape? __________
4. Why does John know he is safe? __________
5. What does John do when he becomes a judge? __________

16 **Play bingo.** Which lines have three correct answers?

1. Cross out three people.
2. Cross out the word that means the same as *dangerous.*
3. Cross out a kind of metal.
4. Cross out the thing that pirates used to attack people with.
5. Cross out the word that means the same as *wrong.*
6. Cross out the thing that ships carry to sell in other countries.

~~captain~~	shipwreck	weapon
cargo	sailor	silver
incorrect	unsafe	iceberg
passenger	impossible	lifeboat

GRAMMAR

It is	fair / unfair		capture animals.
	possible / impossible		ascend this mountain.
	right / wrong	**to**	dive there.
It was	safe / unsafe		explore the cave.
	important / not important		wear safety gear.

17 Look and write. Complete the sentences.

dangerous / touch	possible / visit
illegal / throw	~~safe / swim~~
important / wear	wrong / leave

1. Hey, look! It's safe to swim at this beach.
2. Be careful! ______________ jellyfish.
3. Pick up your trash! ______________ it on the beach.
4. Don't forget! ______________ your life jacket.
5. Don't do that! ______________ trash in the sea.
6. It's ______________ a doctor if you feel sick.

1 2 3
DANGER!
5
WEAR IT!
4
ILLEGAL!
6

18 Work with a partner. Go to page 127. Work with your partner.

19 **Listen.** Number the order in which Joao did these activities. **TR: 62**

1 He made a pot of tea.
___ He invented some clues.
___ He soaked the paper in the tea.
___ He drew a line from one clue to the next.
4 He drew a map of the island.
___ He dried the paper.
8 He cut the paper and folded it many times.
___ He wrote an *X* where the treasure is buried.

Shipwreck Corner
Cargo Cave
Pirate Point
N
W
E
S

20 **Write.** Join the two sentences with as *soon as*.

1. The tea was cold. Joao soaked the paper in it.

   As soon as the tea was cold, Joao soaked the paper in it.

2. The paper was brown. He took it out and left it to dry.

   ___

3. He drew a map on the paper. It was dry.

   ___

4. He drew dotted lines on the map. The clues were prepared.

   ___

5. He finished the map. He cut the paper and folded it.

   ___

21 **Read and write.** Read Joao's notes. Write the missing words.

It's easy to make a pirate map! You should try it! You only have to remember two things: (1) ___ is important ___ soak the paper in the tea for a long time. (2) It ___ necessary to dry the paper completely because if the paper is still wet, ___ impossible ___ write on the map!

22 **Listen and read.** TR: 63

Message in a Bottle

History has many interesting "message in a bottle" stories. In 1915, this famous message was sent by a passenger on the ship *Lusitania*: "Still on deck with a few people. The last boats have left. We are sinking fast. . . . The end is near. . . . Maybe this note will." Another famous message was sent by a Japanese sailor named Matsuyama. His ship sank, but he escaped to a South Pacific island with 43 members of the crew. On the island, he carved a message into wood, put it in a bottle, and placed it in the ocean. It was found in 1935—supposedly in the same Japanese village where Matsuyama was born!

Usually, people sent messages from sinking ships or from desert islands. They were "help" messages and love notes, but the oldest message ever found was different. The bottle, which floated around Scotland for 98 years, belonged to a science experiment by Captain Brown. He wanted to study ocean currents.

Scientist Eddy Carmack also studies ocean currents with bottles. Since 2000, he has sent 6,400 bottled messages from ships around the world. Some have traveled from Mexico to the Philippines; others have traveled from Canada to France. One circled Antarctica one and a half times before it reached Australia. If you find one the next time you are on the beach, be sure to send Carmack an e-mail!

23 **Read and write.** Complete the chart.

People who send messages in bottles	Reasons they send them
passengers on sinking ships	______________
______________	______________
______________	______________

Captain Bercaw dropped two bottles in the same week from the same place in the United States. Both bottles reached France. One arrived a year and a half later. The other took ten years.

 **Look and read.** Draw the journeys on the map. Label them 1-4.

Journeys of Bottled Messages

1. Matsuyama's bottle
2. Carmack's bottle (Mexico to the Philippines)
3. Carmack's bottle (Canada to France)
4. Carmack's bottle (Antarctica to Australia)

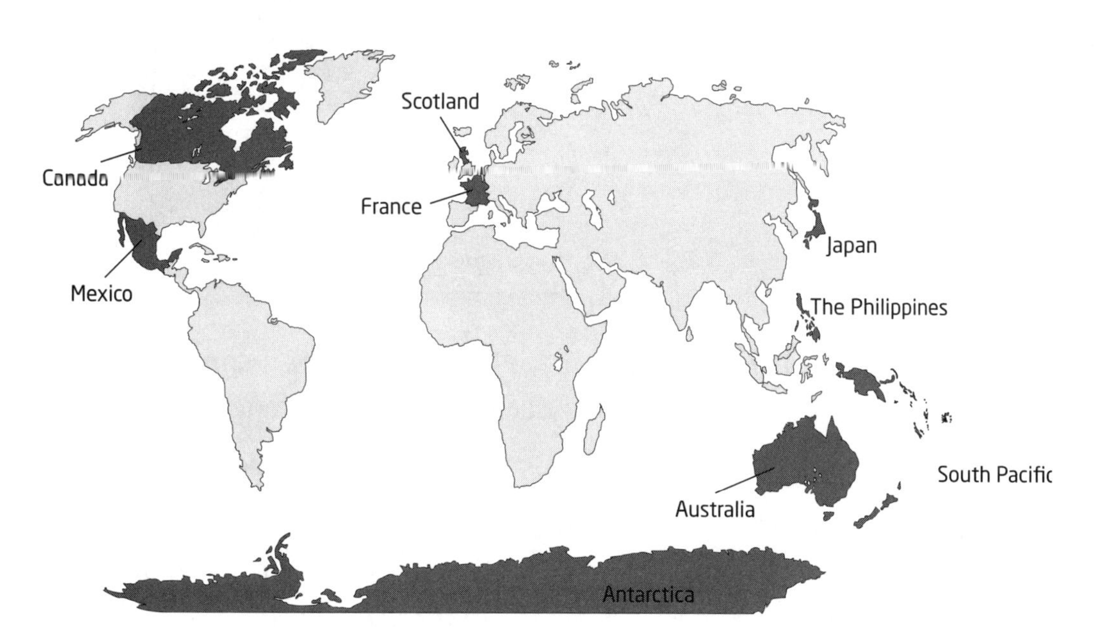

25 Read "between the lines." Underline the correct answer.

1. We are sinking fast. . . . The end is near. . . . Maybe this note will.
   The man who sent this message a. still had hope. b. had no hope.
2. . . . supposedly in the same Japanese village where Matsuyama was born!
   The story of Matsuyama's bottle a. is definitely true. b. could be a legend.
3. The bottle, which floated around Scotland for 98 years. . . .
   The bottle traveled around a. the world. b. one country.

26 Work with a partner. Discuss the questions.

1. In your opinion, which is the most interesting story in the text?
2. Imagine you were on a desert island. What would you write in a message?
3. Imagine you found a message in a bottle. What would you do?

27 **Read *Whose Treasure Is It?* on page 152 of your Student Book.**
How did the writer plan his writing? Read the steps.

1. First, the writer chose a question that has no correct answer. It depends on different points of view. In this case, the silver coins could belong to the United States, Spain, Peru, or no one.
2. Next, the writer wrote down different people's points of view and their reasons. He used a word map.

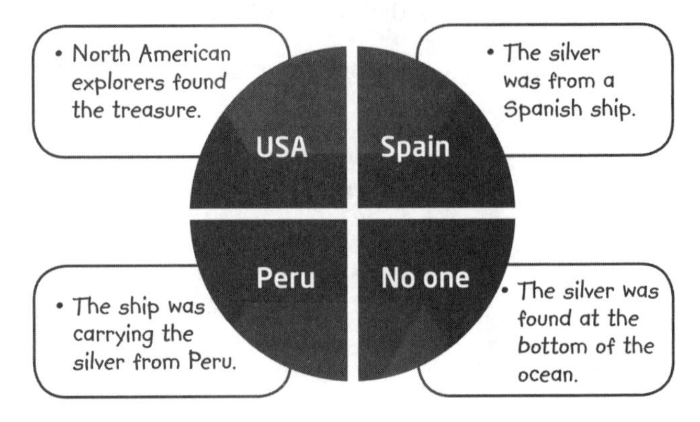

• North American explorers found the treasure.
USA
• The silver was from a Spanish ship.
Spain
Peru
• The ship was carrying the silver from Peru.
No one
• The silver was found at the bottom of the ocean.

3. After he made notes about the treasure, the writer wrote down some key arguments that show a contrast of opinions. Then he decided which sentences to connect.

Sentence 1		Sentence 2
a. The ship was Spanish	BUT	it was carrying Peruvian silver.
b. The silver was from a Spanish ship	BUT	it was made with Peruvian silver.
c. The explorers were from the USA	BUT	there is an agreement with Spain.

4. Then he thought of words and expressions that show concession. This means that the writer accepts that the points of view are all partially correct. He used some common expressions of concession to do this:

   While it may be true that . . . Even though . . . Granted that . . .

   Which words or expressions did the writer use to connect these sentences?

   a. ______________________ the ship was Spanish, it was carrying the silver from Peru.

   b. ______________________ the explorers who discovered the treasure are from the USA, there is an agreement between the USA and Spain stating that all silver from Spanish shipwrecks must go back to Spain.

   c. So ______________________ three countries wanted this treasure, it now belongs to Spain.

5. Finally, he wrote his first version, called a draft, of his paragraph.

28 **Look at Activity 18 in your Student Book.** Think of reasons why the objects could belong to explorers, relatives of survivors, or museums. Follow the steps on page 116. Plan your paragraph. Then write it in your notebook.

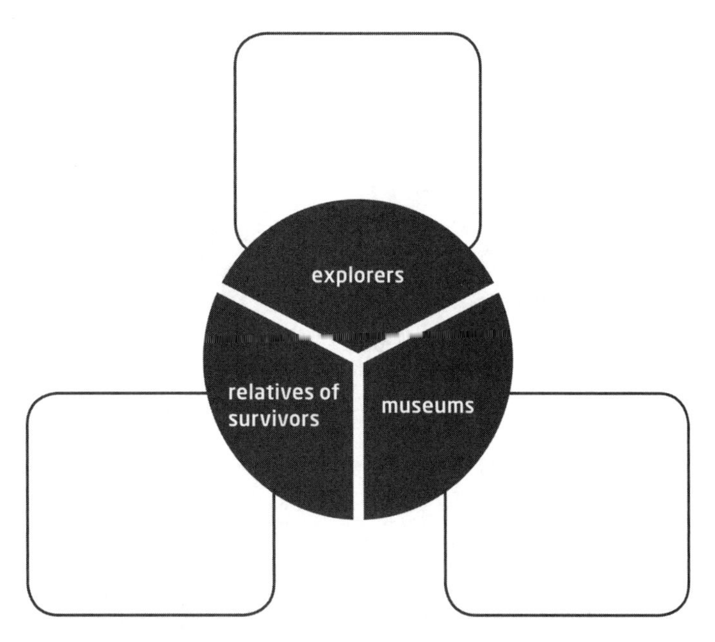

Sentence 1	Sentence 2
a.	BUT
b.	BUT
c.	BUT

29 **Check your writing.** Reread your paragraph carefully!

- Is the paragraph organized clearly?
- Does it have concession sentences?
- Did you include a few opinions?
- Is the spelling correct?

30 **Express yourself.** Choose one of the topics below and write a paragraph of concession. Plan your writing and follow the steps on page 116. Write your new paragraph in your notebook.

If you find money in the street, is it yours?
Is it wrong to put bottled messages in the ocean?
Is it dangerous to travel by sea?

Review

1 **Listen and write.** Listen to the descriptions. Write how it makes each person feel. **TR: 64**

sick

____

____

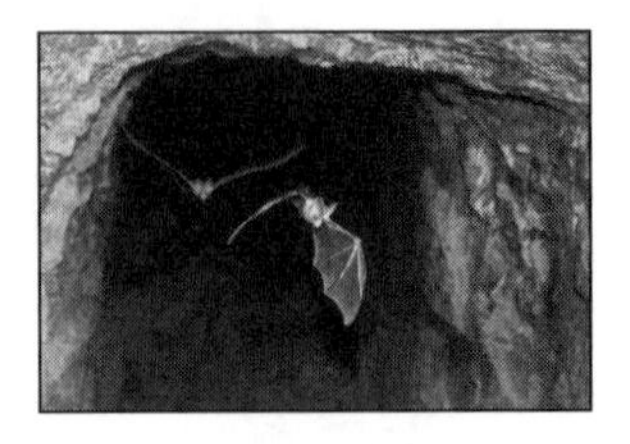
____

____

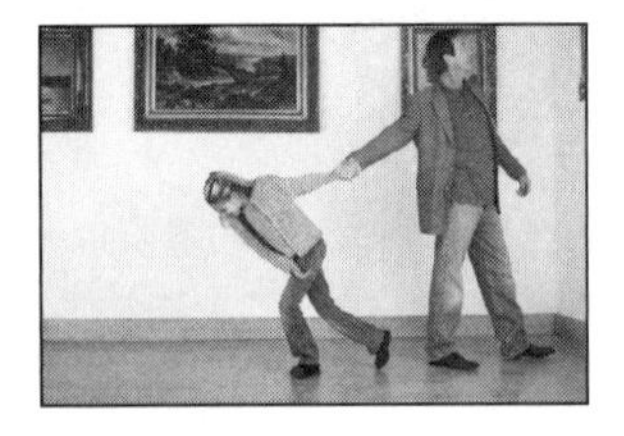
____

____

____

2 **Write.** Make true sentences.

1. Listening to music makes me happy.
2. Science-fiction movies ________.
3. Staying up late at night ________.
4. ________ makes me scared.
5. ________ made me happy.
6. ________ makes me angry.

3 **Read.** Circle the correct word in each sentence.

1. I don't believe that story. I think it's just an old **cargo** / **legend** / **shipwreck**.
2. The **passenger** / **companion** / **captain** usually tells the crew which tasks to do.
3. People escaped the sinking ship in **curiosity** / **lifeboats** / **icebergs**.
4. A long time ago, crews carried weapons to fight **sailors** / **ancestors** / **pirates**.
5. Don't dive here without safety equipment. It's a big **accident** / **risk** / **unsafe**.

4 **Read and write.** Complete the text.

facial recognition ~~features~~ lasers mechanical arm sensors voice recognition

My robot has many interesting ____features____. For example, he has ______________ to help him feel and touch things. He also has ______________, which help him move around without falling over. He knows that you are talking to him because he has excellent ______________. He has amazing ______________, too. He knows your face! My robot has a complex ______________, which helps him pick up objects. When he says goodbye, he waves to you!

5 **Listen.** Listen to the conversation. Choose the correct answer. **TR: 65**

1. Sara wishes she had a _____ robot.	a. social	b. mechanical
2. David would like a _____ for life.	a. program	b. companion
3. Sara's robot will _____ her jokes.	a. make	b. respond to
4. David's robot will be _____ to play video games.	a. told	b. programmed
5. Sara will _____ her robot to do tasks.	a. command	b. control
6. They look on the Internet for _____.	a. ideas	b. information

6 **Read and write.** Write what these people wish.

Me

1. I can't dive.
2. I don't have much curiosity.
3. I trip over things all the time!

My family

4. (Mom) I don't know my ancestors.
5. (Dad) I can't swim underwater.
6. (Brother) I can't speak English.

1. I wish I could dive.
2. ______________________________
3. ______________________________
4. My mom ______________________________.
5. My dad ______________________________.
6. My brother ______________________________.

7 **Read and write.** Complete the sentences.

dangerous / descend   illegal / take   legal / drive   possible / visit   ~~unsafe / travel~~

1. The captain says ___it is unsafe to travel___ near the iceberg.
2. In my country, ______________________ a car when you are 18 years old.
3. ______________________ this mountain. You could have an accident.
4. ______________________ seeds and plants to other countries.
5. I'd like be a sailor. ______________________ many countries with a job like that.

8 **Look and write.** Look at the pictures. Answer the questions.

1 2 3 4

chase – trip over   ~~cross – attack~~   dive – drown   fall – sink

1. Who was crossing the bridge? What happened to him?
   A man was crossing the bridge when some bees attacked him.
2. What fell into the water by accident? Where did the object go?
   ____
3. How did the boy enter the pool? Why?
   ____
4. What was Ana chasing? How did she fall?
   ____

9 **Write.** Continue the sentences. Use *as soon as*.

1. Bats like dark places. They fly away ___as soon as you shine light on them___. (*shine light*)
2. The passengers wanted to swim. They dove into the ocean ______________________. (*safety gear*)
3. The bridge was old and dangerous. It broke ______________________. (*cross*)
4. Some thieves stole the silver. The police took the thieves to jail ______________________. (*capture*)

10 **Read and write.** Complete the sentences.

can / find	can't / locate	~~have to / control~~
must / wear	will / program	won't / teach

1. A robot on the moon has to be controlled by humans with a remote control.
2. Some shipwrecks ________________ because no one knows where they sank.
3. Safety gear ________________ in this cave. It is very important.
4. In the future, robots ________________ to think for themselves.
5. A lot of information ________________ on the Internet. It's really amazing.
6. One day, children ________________ by teachers. Robots will teach them.

11 **Read.** Check **T** for *True* and **F** for *False*.

Cave paintings exist all over the world. Some were painted as long as 40,000 years ago. Many show dangerous animals, and some have *flutings* (lines drawn with human fingers). Caves often have low ceilings, so the artists had to crawl through long dark tunnels on their stomachs. With no safety gear, it was dangerous. Artists shone simple lamps on the walls. Who were these brave people? Between 2000 and 2011, scientists analyzed hundreds of cave paintings in Rouffignac Cave, France. They discovered that many of the flutings were done by children! The flutings, which are about 13,000 years old, are sometimes 2 meters (6.5 feet) high. Did the children's parents lift them up? Why did children draw flutings on the walls? We won't know until we have more information.

1. Cave paintings can only be found in France. (T) (F) ✓
2. Flutings are drawings done with human fingers. (T) (F)
3. It was unsafe for the artists because there were many risks. (T) (F)
4. The height of the French flutings suggests that adults helped the children. (T) (F)
5. Scientists know why children painted the walls. (T) (F)

12 **Write in your notebook.** Today, Rouffignac Cave can be visited by tourists. Would you like to go there? Why or why not?

Unit 3 Student 1, use with Activity 22 on page 33.

22 **Ask and answer.** Look at your chart. Write the questions you need to know.

1. Ask your questions to your partner. Write the answer in your chart.
2. Listen to your partner's questions and answer them. Write the answer in your chart.

What were the Olmec people growing thousands of years ago?

They were growing cacao trees.

Thanks. Now it's my turn to ask another question.

When	Who	What
Example: Thousands of years ago	the Olmec people	What were the Olmec people growing thousands of years ago?
1. As early as 500 C.E.	the people of the Americas	drink / liquid chocolate
2. Between 1200 and 1500	the Aztec people	
3. In the 1850s	an Englishman called Joseph Fry	add / cocoa butter to chocolate
4. In the 1870s	people	
5. As early as 1897	we	make / cookies with the first recipe
6. By 1913	a Swiss man called Sechaud	

Unit 5 Student 1, use with Activity 20 on page 61.

A **Complete the following list of adjectives and words.** Use your own ideas.

1. the name or number of your classroom ____________
2. a number (between 5 and 20) ____________
3. an adjective of shape or size ____________
4. an adjective of age ____________
5. an adjective of size or shape ____________
6. an adjective of pattern ____________
7. an adjective of color ____________
8. an adjective of material ____________
9. a snack you often eat (plural) ____________
10. something you drink (plural) ____________
11. an adjective of size, shape, or material ____________
12. an adjective of size, shape, or material ____________

B **Listen to your partner's adjectives.** Write them in the text below.

"Funny fill-in"

During the school vacation, two fat black hairy spiders were living under a desk in (1) ____________. One day, (2) ____________ schoolchildren arrived for class. "Ugh!" said the male spider. "These school kids are (3) ____________." The female spider replied: "They're (4) ____________ and (5) ____________, aren't they?" Then the male spider spoke again: "My dad said that I should be careful because schoolchildren were dangerous. He said that they had (6) ____________ arms and (7) ____________ (8) ____________ legs." Then the female spider said: "Well, my mom told me something *worse*. She said that humans ate spider (9) ____________ and put our legs in their (10) ____________! Imagine that!" Both spiders suddenly felt scared of the young humans. "Quick, let's go," said the male spider. "I think I prefer to share a room with those (11) ____________ (12) ____________ eyelash mites in the other classroom!"

C **Tell your partner your adjectives.**

D **Read the funny fill-in aloud to your partner.** Then listen to your partner read the funny fill-in with your words. Which one is funnier?

Unit 3 Student 2, use with Activity 22 on page 33.

22 **Ask and answer.** Look at your chart. Write the questions you need to know.

1. Listen to your partner's questions and answer them. Write the answer in your chart.
2. Ask your questions to your partner. Write the answer in your chart.

What were the Olmec people growing thousands of years ago?

They were growing cacao trees.

Thanks. Now it's my turn to ask another question.

When	Who	What
Example: Thousands of years ago	the Olmec people	grow / cacao trees They were growing cacao trees.
1. As early as 500 C.E.	the people of the Americas	
2. Between 1200 and 1500	the Aztec people	use / cocoa beans as money
3. In the 1850s	an Englishman called Joseph Fry	
4. In the 1870s	people	enjoy / the first milk chocolate bar
5. As early as 1897	we	
6. By 1913	a Swiss man called Sechaud	add / fillings to chocolate

Unit 5 Student 2, use with Activity 20 on page 61.

A Complete the following list of adjectives and words. Use your own ideas.

1. the name or number of your classroom ____________
2. a number (between 5 and 20) ____________
3. an adjective of shape or size ____________
4. an adjective of age ____________
5. an adjective of size or shape ____________
6. an adjective of pattern ____________
7. an adjective of color ____________
8. an adjective of material ____________
9. a snack you often eat (plural) ____________
10. something you drink (plural) ____________
11. an adjective of size, shape, or material ____________
12. an adjective of size, shape, or material ____________

B Listen to your partner's adjectives. Write them in the text below.

"Funny fill-in"

During the school vacation, two fat black hairy spiders were living under a desk in (1) ____________. One day, (2) ____________ schoolchildren arrived for class. "Ugh!" said the male spider. "These school kids are (3) ____________." The female spider replied: "They're (4) ____________ and (5) ____________, aren't they?" Then the male spider spoke again: "My dad said that I should be careful because schoolchildren were dangerous. He said that they had (6) ____________ arms and (7) ____________ (8) ____________ legs." Then the female spider said: "Well, my mom told me something *worse*. She said that humans ate spider (9) ____________ and put our legs in their (10) ____________! Imagine that!" Both spiders suddenly felt scared of the young humans. "Quick, let's go," said the male spider. "I think I prefer to share a room with those (11) ____________ (12) ____________ eyelash mites in the other classroom!"

C Tell your partner your adjectives.

D Read the funny fill-in aloud to your partner. Then listen to your partner read the funny fill-in with your words. Which one is funnier?

Unit 6 Student 1, use with Activity 19 on page 73.

19 Work with a partner.

1. Ask your partner about numbers 1, 3, 5, and 7. Ask what the people said.
2. Listen to your partner's answers. Write the sentences in the speech bubbles.
3. Now answer your partner's questions.

Example:

Student 1: What did the girl say in number 1?

Student 2: She asked (him) if he had milk chocolate.

Student 1: So that's "Do you have milk chocolate?"

Student 2: Yes, that's right! Write it in the picture.

Unit 9 Use with Activity 18 on page 112.

18 **Play a game.** Work with your partner, taking turns.

1. Start at the pirate ship. Roll a die, and move that many spaces.
2. If you land at the bottom of a ladder, climb up!
3. If you land at the head of a snake, slide back!
4. If you land in a square with a picture, name it!
5. If you land in a square with a word pair, make a sentence!
6. The first person to the treasure wins.

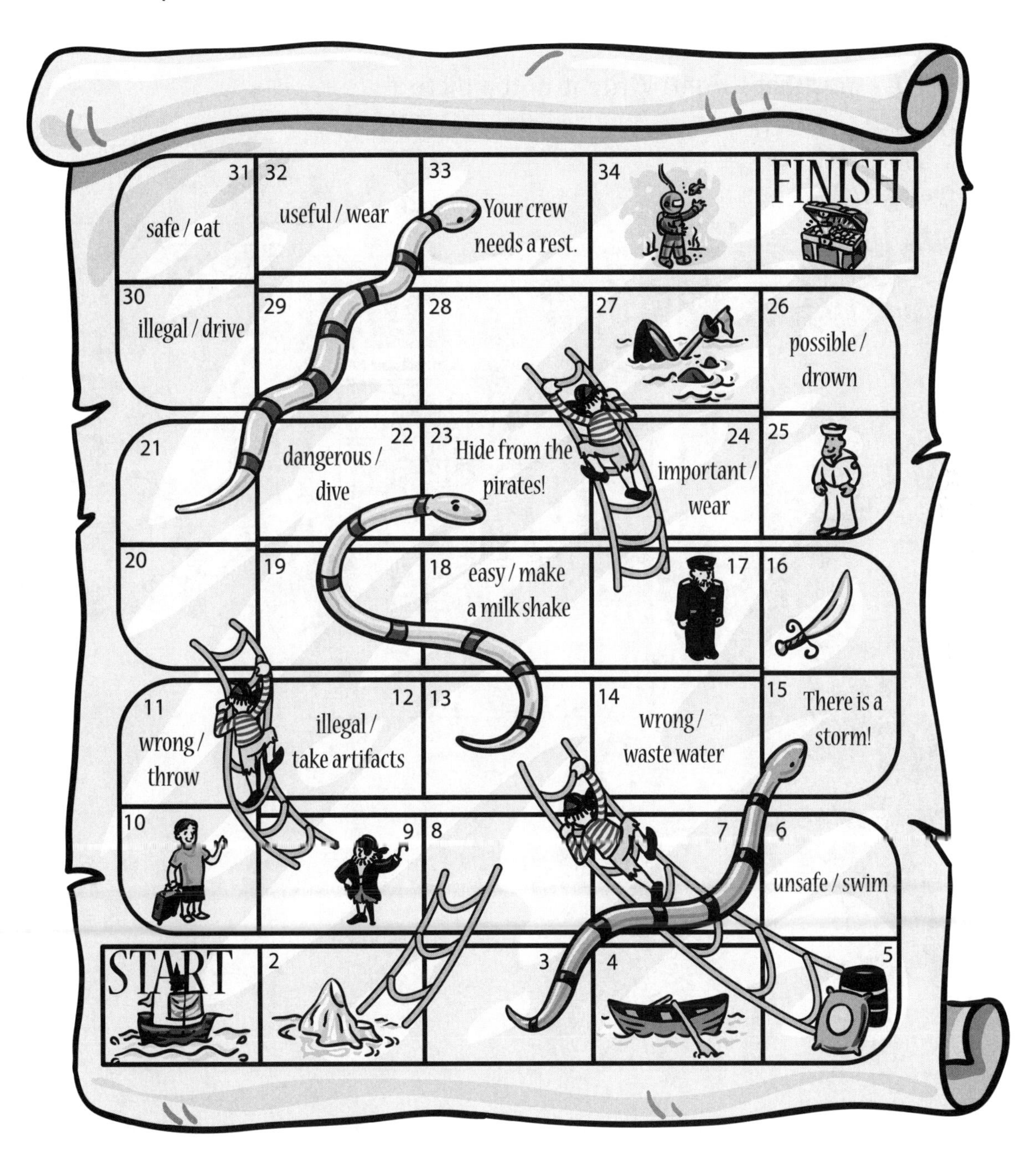

Unit 6 Student 2, use with Activity 19 on page 73.

19 Work with a partner.

1. Answer your partner's questions.
2. Ask your partner about numbers 2, 4, 6, and 8. Ask what the people said.
3. Listen to your partner's answers. Write the sentences in the speech bubbles.

Example:

Student 2 – What did the man say in number 2?

Student 1 – He said he was sorry. He doesn't sell that.

Student 2 – So that's "I'm sorry. I don't sell that"?

Student 1 – Yes, that's right! Write it in the picture.